THE ULTIMATE GUIDE to Writing MODERN Cozy Murder Mysteries

HOW TO WRITE A COZY MYSTERY

NINA HARRINGTON

HOW TO WRITE A COZY MYSTERY

THE ULTIMATE GUIDE TO WRITING MODERN COZY MURDER MYSTERIES

NINA HARRINGTON

HOW TO WRITE A COZY MYSTERY

THE ULTIMATE GUIDE TO WRITING MODERN COZY MURDER MYSTERIES

COPYRIGHT© 2021 NINA HARRINGTON. All rights reserved.

ISBN: 978-0-9571289-7-2.

No part of this publication may be reproduced or transmitted in any form or by any means, mechanical or electronic, including photocopying and recording, or by any information storage and retrieval systems, without permission in writing from the author.

The content of this book is provided for educational purposes. Every effort has been made to ensure the accuracy of the information presented. However, the information is sold without warranty, either express or implied, and the author shall not be liable for any loss or damage caused, whether directly or indirectly, by its use.

Attribution. The authors of extracts used in this book hold full copyright on their work.

Thanks to Nancy Warren for giving permission to use an extract from: The Vampire Knitting Club.

Thanks to Implode Publishing Ltd for granting permission to use an extract from: Witch is When It All Began.

A Note on Terminology. Although I am from the UK and this book is written in UK English, for the sake of consistency this book uses the US spelling of "cozy" mystery which has been widely accepted as universal.

NinaHarringtonDigital.

https://ninaharrington.com/

Contents

INTRODUCTION 3

THE MODERN COZY MURDER MYSTERY 5
THE TEN KEY ELEMENTS OF A MODERN COZY MYSTERY 6
THE MARKET FOR COZY MYSTERY FICTION 18
WHAT IS YOUR NICHE? 29
THE IDEAL WORDCOUNT FOR MODERN COZY MYSTERIES 39

THE THREE HOOKS AND A SLEUTH STORY GENERATOR 47
THE THREE HOOKS AND A SLEUTH STORY GENERATOR 48
PRE-WRITING EXERCISES 61

FOUR ACT STORY STRUCTURE 63
HOW TO USE STORY STRUCTURE 64
MURDER MYSTERY STORY STRUCTURE 69

COZY MYSTERY PLOT TEMPLATE 71

HOW TO WRITE THE FIRST DRAFT IN TEN STEPS 96
How to Use the Ten-Step Process 98
STEP ONE. Expand the 3 Hooks and a Sleuth idea 99
STEP TWO. Decide on your Target Wordcount 102
STEP THREE. Point of View 104
STEP FOUR. Creating a Memorable Sleuth 111
STEP FIVE. The First Murder Victim 124
STEP SIX. The Suspects 129

STEP SEVEN. The Murderer 135

STEP EIGHT. Use Scene Cards to write a First Draft of Act One. 141

Act One. Sequence 1. The Sleuth in their Ordinary World 150

Act One Sequence 2. The Inciting Incident 151

Act One Sequence 3. Reaction to the Murder 152

Act One Sequence 4. The Sleuth Commits to the Investigation 153

STEP NINE. Sanity Check after writing the Opening Scenes 155

STEP TEN. Write down Ideas for the next Key Plot Turning Points   156

WRITING A CONTINUITY SERIES 159

WRITING A MYSTERY SERIES 160

CASE STUDY DECONSTRUCTION 167

Chapter One 168

SUMMARY 189

FREE BONUS ADDITIONAL RESOURCES 190

THANK YOU 191

ABOUT THE AUTHOR 192

INTRODUCTION

Thank you for selecting this ultimate guide on how to write a modern cozy murder mystery.

Like you, I love reading crime fiction, including both thrillers and cozy murder mysteries, and have a large personal library of *whodunit* novels on my physical and electronic "keeper shelves".

For the past 20 years, I have also been a student of story structure. My goal is simple. I want to understand how I can apply story craft to shape a story idea into compelling commercial fiction that will appeal to my ideal target audience.

With this book, I have consolidated my extensive personal notes and reference material on story craft to create a resource you can dip into whenever you need additional information on a specific aspect of developing a cozy mystery novel.

I will be covering all aspects of writing a modern commercial cozy murder mystery novel or screenplay, from developing the concept through to story structure for full-length fiction, including how to use subplots, secondary characters and building a series.

Each chapter is supported by worked examples, outlines, templates and professional writing tips and techniques. Writing exercises are included where appropriate.

Each writer is unique and has their own process. But whether you are an intuitive author who writes themselves into a story, or a plotter who creates a working outline before they create the text, at some point you will need to edit and rework your cozy mystery manuscript into the most effective story form possible.

Two things, however, are clear.

Firstly, the most popular form of cozy mysteries are murder mysteries.

Secondly, this subgenre of popular fiction has unwritten story conventions, tropes, and elements that today's readers will both recognize and expect to see in modern cozy mystery fiction.

Why Modern Commercial Cozy Mysteries?

It is perfectly fine if you want to create a cozy mystery for your own enjoyment and have fun doing so. But why not share your work with other readers who love cozy mysteries as much as you do?

There will always be readers who love golden age mysteries from writers such as Dorothy L. Sayers and Agatha Christie, but there is also a large demand for modern cozy mystery fiction around the world where the sleuth can be a witch, an animal, or a vampire. Or perhaps a combination of all three! Cross-genre, high-concept cozy mysteries have become very popular and provide a perfect escapist journey for the reader.

This wide variety of new niche subcategories in the cozy mystery genre means that there are readers online at this moment, looking for precisely the kind of cozy that you love to read and are planning to write. From historical to contemporary, paranormal to small town, there are readers who have a passion for niche cozy mystery fiction. That is why this book has a section on how to understand the market for cozy mysteries and how you can use that data to find an audience for your work.

My sincere hope is that this book will guide you through the expectations and key elements of cozy mystery fiction and how you can write a compelling story that both hits the expected story beats and remains unique.

No fluff or padding. Just practical information so that you can write your commercial modern cozy murder mystery – fast!

THE MODERN COZY MURDER MYSTERY

THE TEN KEY ELEMENTS OF A MODERN COZY MYSTERY

Just like any other form of fiction, it is important to understand who will be reading your cozy mystery, and, as a result, what they will be looking for.

Who is your ideal reader? Do you have a clear picture in your mind of the person you are writing for?

Convention tells us that cozy mystery readers are overwhelmingly female, based in the United States and aged 40 years and above. This is, of course, a generalization, but works as a useful avatar that you can use to understand your ideal readers and their expectations.

What do readers expect to find when they buy a cozy murder mystery?

The author/publisher is making a very specific promise to the reader when they describe a novel as a cozy mystery.

Readers, just like us, expect to be taken on a unique type of emotional and intellectual journey through the pages of a cozy mystery and that promise needs to be stated on the cover, in the book description and then delivered on the page.

For me, that emotional experience that a cozy mystery should deliver is made up of ten key elements.

1. Humour

For me, humour is an essential component of any cozy mystery, and I expect to discover a light-hearted entertaining read.

There is enough gloom and negativity in the real world around us.

Readers pick up a cozy mystery so that they can escape into another world inside the pages of your book.

Most cozy mysteries have a fun, light tone to balance out the darkness of the murder investigations. There may be witty banter between the sleuth and the sidekick and supporting characters or a funny pet or animal or fun situations and dilemmas arising from character traits, supernatural acts, and family interactions.

2. Family-Friendly Content

Cozy murder mysteries are classified as "clean" family-friendly books, so readers don't expect to see bad language, racism, blasphemy, drug addition, abuse or violence against children or animals. Even from the killer!

If there is a romance subplot the bedroom door should remain firmly closed. These are not the books for sexually explicit or sexually intimate scenes.

There may be action and even dangerous scenes where the sleuth and the sidekick are in peril as a result of their investigations, but they will not be permanently injured.

In particular, you should avoid the kind of forensic descriptions of crime scenes, gory murder details or graphic violence that you can find in police procedurals, forensic TV shows or mainstream crime books and thrillers.

3. An Interesting Setting or Situation

These novels take the reader away from day-to-day troubles into interesting story worlds. Most include small town settings and/or historical time periods which have layers of familiar details that readers will recognize.

These add to the warm feelings of charm, nostalgia and community connections that come with your setting.

Classic murder mysteries were frequently set in remote locations such as English country houses, run-down large hotels, long-distance trains, cruise ships and islands.

In other words, locations where the entire cast is contained in one place for the length of the novel, free from interference from the local police force.

The murderer, victims, sleuths, and sidekicks were trapped inside a physical pressure cooker of a situation from which they were physically unable to escape. They cannot call for help when one of them is murdered. Phone lines are down. Power may be out. They are forced to investigate and find the killer alone.

This technique is still used in many murder mystery crime novels, TV shows and movies.

For example. **Private Eyes** TV show episode S2 E12. **Getaway with Murder.** There is a violent snow blizzard, and a luxury ski resort is cut-off from the outside world when the hotel owner is found murdered.

Or, as in the 2019 movie **Knives Out,** the family are assembled at the remote family home to celebrate the 85th birthday of the rich patriarch, when he is found dead the next morning.

The same theme has been used by authors Lucy Foley in her novel **The Guest List** and A. M. Castle in **The Invitation**.

Many cozy mysteries are set in small towns and/or rural or seaside locations where they don't have access to professional homicide units and forensic teams – they may have one under-resourced police team and a local doctor. Tourists and visitors are rare and the murder victim within this small local community clearly knew his or her killer.

Alternatively, a cozy mystery can be set in an area of a larger town or city where there is an equivalent close community of connected individuals who unite to investigate the murder of one of their members.

For example. In Richard Osman's **The Thursday Murder Club,** the murder takes place in a luxury English retirement village.

This connected group of people simulates the closed country house scenario with an insider knowledge of the location and the local characters. They can then use those insights to find the killer.

4. An Interesting Story Theme

Themes and hooks act as instant short-cuts which quickly tell the reader exactly what kind of story they should expect on the page.

Both the theme and the hook of your work must be attractive to your target audience and automatically signal the charm and nostalgic emotional appeal that your readers will be looking for in a particular niche.

Cozy Mystery Themes
- **Animals**
- **Crafts and Hobbies**
- **Culinary**
- **Historical Settings**
- **Paranormal and Supernatural**

These themes should not distract from the central murder investigation, but add to the worldbuilding and character development for the sleuth and secondary characters.

The theme can then be used to classify your book as falling into a specific niche cozy mystery market.

Most commercially successful cozy mysteries have an ongoing theme which adds interesting layers of depth to the storyline and provides for subplots.

These themes provide new information to the reader about a craft or a skill or hobby that they may not be familiar with.

The main themes are generally classified in physical bookstores and online retailers such as the Amazon store as:

Animal Cozy Mysteries

Does your book include farm animals or pets such as cats and dogs?

Readers love murder mysteries which include house pets, and they are always pictured on the cover of the book.

Cats and kittens seem to be the top sellers, then dogs followed by pets and farm animals. The animal could also be the sleuth, complete with animal sidekicks!

Crafts and Hobbies Cozy Mysteries

Does your sleuth have a particular profession, hobby or interest which could be used as a theme?

For example, the sleuth could own an old inn, run a knitting shop, be a member of a crochet and quilting circle, design couture wedding gowns and hats or work in an art supply shop. Needlecraft hobbies are particularly popular.

What if your sleuth loves to take ballroom dancing or bookbinding classes? Or perhaps she works as a part time pet sitter for friends and neighbours?

She might adore making theatre costumes, rummage around in antique shops and go to belly dancing classes at the weekends.

The list of possibilities is endless, which makes this subcategory very exciting. There is always room for something new!

Culinary Cozy Mysteries

Food and drink themed mysteries are still as popular as ever. This subcategory includes anything from bakeries, cupcake shops, ice cream parlours, bistros, cafes, coffee shops, restaurants, food vans and wine merchants right through to wedding caterers and private chefs. This is a huge subcategory which allows lots of room for new examples with a fresh twist.

Historical Settings

Most popular murder mysteries are contemporary. Readers love to identify with the sleuth and their situation in a small modern community and can see themselves in that character. From the author's point of view this also makes research a lot easier.

The golden age for murder mysteries began in the interwar years in the 1920s and 1930s and this time period is still very popular with readers.

There is a huge range of popular historical murder mysteries set in Edwardian or 1930s England. For example, the Lady Hardcastle Mysteries from T.E. Kinsey and the Lady Eleanor Swift Mystery Series from Verity Bright, and there are many more.

Solving the murder without the aid of the internet and technology means that the sleuth must be particularly skilled, competent, and able to work within the confines of the strict social structures and moral standards of that time.

Extensive research is needed to make these murder mysteries both convincing and emotionally appealing to a modern reader, and the historical details of specific settings must also be meticulously accurate. For example, the practical implications of transport conditions using horse drawn carriages on unpaved roads in rural settings or ocean crossings on early steam ships have to feel real.

Paranormal and Supernatural Mysteries

Cross-over cozy mysteries involving paranormal and supernatural elements such as witches, ghosts, magic, psychic and vampire storylines are becoming an increasingly large part of this genre and there are numerous very successful series using these themes.

The nature of these themes means that you can use elements from these other genres to support the detective and the investigation. They must, of course, be reasonable, believable, and logical within the rules of the story world that you have created for the characters and the murder investigation.

5. A Compelling and Different Story Hook

I like to think that the "hook" of your story is that unique aspect which a cozy mystery reader will instantly recognize as the KEY that unlocks your story world.

For me, the hook is an additional story element that is linked to the theme.

The most successful hooks are what is known as **"high concept".**

A high concept idea is an idea that can be pitched in one sentence and immediately conveys why it's cool or interesting.

Example One. In **Kitty Confidential by Molly Fitz,** the sleuth has an electric shock from a faulty coffee machine and wakes up to find that she can understand the only witness to a murder – the victim's cat.

The theme is: Animal Cozy Mystery.

The hook is: the sleuth is a Pet Whisperer and the victim's cat helps her to discover who murdered its owner.

Example Two. In **The Vampire Knitting Club by Nancy Warren,** the sleuth has inherited her grandmother's knitting shop, then discovers that her grandmother was murdered then rescued by a group of vampires.

The theme is: Crafts and Hobbies Cozy Mystery. Knitting is a key part of the storyline.

Second theme: Paranormal Vampire Mysteries.

The hook is: the sleuth discovers that she is a witch and works with vampires who live below her knitting shop to investigate the murder of her grandmother.

Vampires who live below a knitting shop? That is cool, different, and interesting.

6. Each Cozy is a Complete Murder Mystery Puzzle

Cozy murder mysteries have a puzzle to solve. There will be at least one murder and often two linked murders in a full-length murder mystery novel.

The murder or other serious crime will usually happen in the first quarter of the book and generate a number of questions which will be answered by the end.

The rest of the book will then track how the sleuth finds the answers to those questions, starting with how this person was killed, why now and then who the killer is.

The murder should be treated with the shock and horror that it deserves. This serves to build the suspense and tension in the story.

Readers like to follow the clues and work out **whodunnit** before or with the sleuth.

This means that all the clues and revelations must be included, but there will also be multiple suspects, red herrings, and distractions for the reader to work through.

This is not the place for detailed descriptions of forensic analyses and the work of large teams of homicide detectives and scene of crime investigators who have limitless resources available to them.

The investigation by our usually amateur sleuth is more cerebral than forensic.

There will be a satisfying conclusion where justice is seen to be done and order restored where the murderer is caught and punished.

The story ends with the arrest of the killer after a dramatic final confrontation, then leaves it there. Law trials and prison scenes are for other types of more hard-boiled crime novels.

David Baldacci, the best-selling crime author, said the genre fits the turbulent political times. "*People inherently don't like folks who do bad to get away with it. In real life they do. But in novels evil is punished and the good guys mostly win,*" he said.

7. An Amateur Sleuth

Note: For the sake of convenience, I am using an example of a female sleuth throughout this book but of course the sleuth could be any gender or creature.

The crime is solved by someone who is an ordinary member of the community.

Our sleuth should be a realistic character that readers can identify with, who may reluctantly agree to get involved, but who has the skills and talents to see the clues, analyse the evidence and solve the crime through common sense and her personal intuition.

The investigation should be well motivated and credible from the start.

These are ordinary people dropped into extraordinary situations by circumstances outside their control and there should be a personal reason why the sleuth is compelled to investigate this murder.

- Why should she put herself into the path of a murderer?
- Does the murder take place in her community or her place of work, for example?
- Or does it impact a close family member who she knows to be innocent of the murder?

The sleuth is usually a woman who runs a business or has a hobby or skill that brings her into close contact with other members of her community.

The sleuth must be able to investigate the crime scene and identify possible suspects because of her knowledge of the community and then interpret clues and revelations based on her background knowledge and personal experience.

To support the sleuth, she may know someone in that community who is linked to professional law enforcement, such as a police officer or private investigator. Someone who can find out the kind of information she cannot access.

The sleuth is going to be the driving force for this book and other books if you plan to create a series of linked novels in the same storyworld, so it is imperative that you spend time working on the background for this character and understand what she wants to achieve at the moment the story opens, her long held desires that have yet to be fulfilled, and her fears and conflicts.

The objective should always be to make the readers sympathize and empathize with the sleuth in the crucial opening scenes. They will be stepping into her shoes and following her thoughts and feelings for the rest of their journey.

The sleuth must be likeable, even if she does have idiosyncrasies of her own. Otherwise, how can the reader identify with her?

One of the reasons why cozy mystery series are so very popular is that the sleuth often has a personal subplot running in the background which is not resolved in full until the end of the series.

8. A Well-motivated Murderer who is a match for our Sleuth.

The story is driven by the murderer. The first murder may have been planned for a long time in advance or be triggered by the actions of the victim, but it is always well motivated.

Psychopaths and sociopaths are rare in cozy mysteries. In most cases, the killer has specifically targeted their victim for a very good reason.

Either way, the murderer's plan to escape detection and justice should be clever enough to be a real challenge to our sleuth, and keep the reader guessing about who did it and why they did it.

This is why some mystery authors start with the killer and develop a detailed outline of who the murder victims are, the motivation for their deaths and how the killer plans to evade justice. This makes sure that the sleuth can be taken down multiple side-tracks but will always find the crucial clues that will lead them to the real murderer.

9. Quirky Sidekicks, Friends and Family

The story will connect the reader with feelings of emotional charm and possibly nostalgia. There is usually a strong sense of the local community and family relationships, backed up by the sleuth's network of friends.

The cast list will include quirky characters that make readers smile if not laugh out loud. This cast of secondary characters will continue across all the books in a continuity series, so that readers can get to know these characters and connect with their lives in this community and/or family. Returning to a series should feel like revisiting old friends you love to spend time with.

Animals and pets can add to the charm and familiarity.

For example. **In Pork Pie Pandemonium: Albert Smith's Culinary Capers** by Steve Higgs, the sleuth's dog is a former police dog who was fired because of his bad attitude. In some scenes, the point of view character switches from the sleuth, Albert Smith, to the dog's point of view at critical points in the murder investigation. The dog acts as a narrator and becomes a real character.

10. Authenticity

There is one further element that is fundamentally important for anyone considering writing a cozy mystery and one that is often overlooked: **a deep and sincere love of this genre.**

For me, it would be impossible to create a convincing and engaging cozy murder mystery if I did not enjoy these stories and want to spend time with the characters and their story worlds.

Cozy murder mystery readers are astute and prolific readers who will easily spot an author who is not taking the genre seriously and creating their best work in a specific cozy niche.

With that in mind, let's move on and understand the current market for cozy murder mystery fiction.

THE MARKET FOR COZY MYSTERY FICTION

Why is it so important to understand the market for cozy mysteries?

Now is the time to ask yourself two key questions:

Why do you want to write cozy mystery, and

What kind of mystery do you love to read and write? What is your niche?

Why do you want to write modern cozy mysteries?

Be honest with yourself.

How you approach writing your cozy mystery depends on understanding the reason why you want to write in this genre and what you want to do with the book when it is complete. For example:

- Do you want to make a living from independently publishing your cozy mysteries as a side-hustle or a full-time writing business?
- Do you want to create a cozy mystery novel and pitch it to a literary agent so they can share your work with editors at publishing houses who will take over the publishing and distribution of your work?
- Do you want to make a mark on society with a unique style or commentary? Perhaps to leave a legacy with the stories that you have been burning to tell.
- Do you simply enjoy writing for its own sake and want to share your stories around the world and the sales are a bonus?
- Or something else? Is this a fun experiment with something different and exciting? Are you taking risks and plan to take the reader somewhere new?

- Do you believe that you are writing for yourself and then hope other cozy mystery book readers will discover your work when the book is finished?

There is no right or wrong path. This has to your individual journey.

But one thing is true.

Way too many fiction authors write the book they want to write and THEN think about how they are going to share that book, market and promote their work and hopefully persuade friends and family to leave a review on the Amazon book page. This only leads to frustration and disappointment and more than a little heartbreak.

"Hope" book marketing is not a strategy for success, no matter what your personal definition of success is.

A far better way is to know in advance that there are readers for the cozy mysteries that you love to read and want to write, and you have the tools and techniques which will help your work to be discovered by ideal readers.

DECIDE ON THE BEST PUBLISHING MODEL FOR YOU AND YOUR WORK.

What can we do as authors to build careers as published authors?

We need to become more prolific and we need to be both educated and business-minded about what is the best publishing model for our work while trying to stand upright on the shifting sand that is today's publishing industry.

How do the top self-published fiction authors make money?

By treating their writing as a business, where they are in control of every aspect of the book publishing process.

They are "authorpreneurs" who see their love of writing as a start-up business opportunity and are prepared to put in the hours of hard work to make it a successful business, however you define what that success looks like.

To become a successful author in the crowded mystery fiction marketplace, I believe that you must learn how to write, edit, produce, publish, and promote your work so that readers know where to find it.

In other words, you need to develop the mindset of a book publisher.

This means releasing at least four or more books a year, preferably in a series, and slowly building a following so that the next book in the series, or a new series, becomes an auto-buy for readers.

That's one of the reasons why many cozy mystery authors prefer to write shorter novels of 50,000 words or fewer. These books are designed to be fast-paced, page-turning reads delivering a fun and escapist read that can be enjoyed in a few hours.

That is not to say that independent publishing is an easy option.

When a reader purchases your book with their precious hard-earned money, they want to enjoy a professionally produced mystery story with the same quality standards that they would find in a printed book from a traditional publisher.

It is all too easy to feel overwhelmed by how much we have to know about story craft, editing, productivity, the publishing business, and how to become business savvy as a writer entrepreneur.

Building an author platform and readership take time and patience. This is not a quick and easy way to make money. You must accept that you are going to be in the online publishing business for the long haul.

Most of the top commercial genre fiction authors have been writing and publishing for at least five to ten years, building up a back-list of books which are selling every day while they are working on the next new release.

For eBooks, it is now well established that if a reader loves one of your books, then they will want to purchase other books that you have created, especially if these books are linked in some way.

The books need to be online and available at that precise moment. Because if you don't have books available, then the opportunity is lost, and the reader with a short attention span will move on to the next author who does have a trilogy or more, all ready to be enjoyed. Right now. Speed is everything.

Visibility and platform = sales.

Getting noticed in the genre fiction publishing business has never been harder. Do not go down the self-publishing route unless you are prepared to invest a significant amount of time in marketing online and off. You will be fighting hard to attract your ideal reader in an extremely competitive marketplace.

Self-publishing any book requires a significant investment in time and money and most of the process has nothing to do with creative writing.

Every part of this process takes time, energy, and money from the start.

So, how badly do you want this?

How much time can you invest in publishing your work? One hour a day is a great place to start but you can achieve a lot more than you imagine in thirty-minute sessions.

In many cases, self-publishing may not be the best publishing model for your book project and skillset.

Not everyone has the desire to create a start-up small publishing company.

If that is the case, there are numerous digital-first publishers and traditional publishers who will take over the publishing side of the business while you handle the writing, but you will still have to do a lot of the marketing and engage a literary agent to represent you.

That's why I believe that time spent researching the sales market for the kind of fiction you want to write is never wasted. In fact, it can save you time, energy, money, and heartache.

Your goal is simple. To learn about your potential customers/ideal readers and understand what they are buying and what they are interested in.

So, with that in mind, let's look at the market for cozy mysteries.

The Global Mystery, Thriller and Suspense Market

Have you ever read a totally enthralling murder mystery novel and been so carried away with the characters and their story world, that when you turned the last page you asked yourself; "*I wonder if I could write a mystery like that?*"

Mystery, thriller and suspense fiction is the second highest-selling genre in the Kindle Store in the United States after romance fiction. Sales have never been greater, and readers are looking for mystery fiction in all sub-categories and lengths to satisfy their compulsion for this genre.

The good news for writers is there has never been a better time to create your own cozy mystery stories and find readers who will enjoy them. Sales of cozy mysteries on the Amazon.com Kindle store, for example, have been increasing year on year for the past five years.

One of the reasons for the universal popularity of cozy crime fiction is that there is now a huge range of story lines for readers to enjoy, covering a full spectrum of story hooks, settings, themes, and cross-genre elements to meet the tastes of every reader.

This diversity means that there truly is a cozy mystery story for every audience – and for any writer. This sub-genre offers writers very special opportunities to explore stories and characters which are as unique as their imagination can take them. But that enormous diversity creates a problem.

Imagine walking into a bookstore and finding stacks of books of all types all piled up together without any kind of order. It would be impossible to find the book you are looking for without sorting through hundreds of random books.

To make it easier, online bookstores such as Amazon have created a range of virtual bookshelves called Categories where readers can go to find the kind of eBooks and printed books that they love to read. This is the online equivalent to labelled shelves in a bricks and mortar bookstore.

Image credit: flickr/pfala

Throughout this book I will using the Amazon.com USA Kindle eBook store as the reference online bookstore for cozy mystery books. Why? Because it is the largest online bookstore in the world. As a result, it is often the first place that cozy mystery readers visit when they are looking for a new title in a specific niche.

Amazon operates as a powerful search engine where readers can find the ideal mystery they are looking for.

Amazon operates as a powerful search engine and if you want to succeed as a cozy mystery writer, your work should be listed on the Amazon bookstore.

A book does not have to be exclusive to Amazon, but if you want readers to discover your work then I would strongly recommend loading your book onto the Amazon platform.

Discoverability is crucial.

You may have to drill down several layers to find the perfect category home for the book that you want to write and fully appreciate what readers are looking for in that niche. Readers must know that your work exists before they can admire your quality book cover and buy and read your book.

Your target readers are looking for a specific type of book and can describe it in the same terms that Amazon uses.

Question. How can you help your ideal reader to find your book on the virtual shelves?

Answer. By being strategic from the start and writing the cozy mystery story that you want to write, but with a clear understanding of how you are going to distribute that book so that the audience for that story is going to find your work.

In other words, you must know precisely which subcategories or sub-subcategories are the target virtual shelves for your mystery on the Kindle store.

You have to love reading and writing that kind of story.

That is a given. After all, you are going to be building up an audience and a following for your work online, and your readers will expect you to continue writing in that niche, even if it is not as popular as it was six months ago.

I am not saying that writing to market is the only way to be successful. Far from it. But it is one example of authors who have:

- proactively identified that there is an audience for their work in advance,

- they enjoy writing those stories, and

- they have stories which will fit that niche market.

They know that there is an existing large audience for their work, so they are not "writing into the blue" then hoping that someone will buy and read their eBook apart from their friends and family.

The story still must be well-crafted with compelling characters, so that readers will enjoy the work, but it also has to meet the genre expectations of that particular sub-genre.

How does Amazon help readers to find their ideal cozy mysteries?

In the Amazon.com (USA) Kindle eBook store you will find Cozy Mysteries filed as a specific subcategory on the **Mystery Virtual Shelf** under **Mystery, Thriller and Suspense.**

Kindle eBooks. Mystery, Thriller & Suspense, then Mystery.

Within Mystery you will currently find books listed under: African American. Amateur Sleuth. Collections & Anthologies. Cozy. Hard-Boiled. Historical. International Mystery & Crime. LGBT. Police Procedurals. Private Investigators. Series. Traditional Detectives. Women Sleuths

Let's focus on Mystery, Thriller and Suspense>Mystery>Cozy.

And within the Cozy subcategory there are three sub-subcategories.

Mystery, Thriller and Suspense>Mystery>Cozy>Culinary.

Mystery, Thriller and Suspense>Mystery>Cozy>Crafts and Hobbies.

Mystery, Thriller and Suspense>Mystery >Cozy>Animals.

Notice that there are also separate subcategories/virtual bookshelves for:

Mystery, Thriller and Suspense >Mystery>Amateur Sleuths.

This is the favourite classification for many murder mysteries, especially those that may not fit perfectly into other subcategories. Independent publishers, small presses and traditional publishers are all represented here. This is the perfect category to find new readers and discover new titles.

Mystery, Thriller and Suspense>Mystery>Women Sleuths and

Mystery, Thriller and Suspense>Mystery>Private Investigators.

Many commercial bestselling crime novels from traditional publishers feature female sleuths and private detectives and these subcategories are dominated by mainstream crime writers such as Greg Olsen, Ann Cleeves, Rachel Caine, J D Robb and Lisa Grey which makes it difficult for murder mystery titles to gain traction.

Mystery, Thriller and Suspense>Mystery>Historical.

The golden age of murder mysteries is listed here, such as the Lord Peter Wimsey Mysteries by Dorothy L. Sayers, works by Ellis Peters and Ken Follett, but there are fewer titles in this subcategory and writers of historical murder mysteries are a perfect fit for this classification.

Mystery, Thriller and Suspense>Mystery>Traditional Detectives and

Mystery, Thriller and Suspense>Crime> Murder Fiction. These subcategories include Sherlock Holmes right through to modern police procedurals.

Cozy mysteries are also included in other categories on the Amazon.com Kindle store, including **Literature and Fiction>Women's Fiction>Mystery, Thriller and Suspense.**

There is therefore considerable overlap and cross-over with elements in cozy mysteries, but books in these subcategories may not conform to the ten-point personal definition of cozy mysteries I described earlier.

There is one trend which is not included in the Cozy Mystery listing – and that is the **Paranormal theme.**

Murder mysteries with paranormal and supernatural themes are now extremely popular. They include murder investigations that involve paranormal elements and characters, such as witches, vampires, ghosts, and psychics.

You will find that most paranormal cozy mysteries have a second or third theme which ensures that they are listed in one of the three main cozy mystery subcategories – animals, crafts and hobbies and culinary.

Amazon also has a separate subcategory under Mystery-Suspense for Supernatural and Paranormal mysteries.

The search path is: **Kindle Store ‹ Kindle eBooks ‹ Mystery, Thriller & Suspense-Suspense, then Ghosts, Horror, Occult, Paranormal, Political or Psychological.**

If you select **Paranormal, there are sub-subcategories for: Psychics, Vampires and Werewolves and Shifters.**

How Competitive is Your Cozy Mystery Niche?

Before you dive into the detailed marketing research, it is always useful to consider how many other books are already listed in the category where your book is the perfect fit.

These books are both your competition and an indication of the popularity of that niche subgenre.

You should always focus on two things:

Factor #1. What subgenre is the most relevant and the best fit for the books you love to read and write.

Where can you find the kind of mysteries that you love to read? Where are they placed on the Kindle store?

Factor #2. How competitive that category is. How many other eBooks are published in that category? This should give you an indication of the level of demand for your kind of book.

A quick way to calculate how hard it would be to dominate a category is see how much competition there is within that category, which is reflected in the ranking of the books in that category.

How Many Books are currently classified as Cozy Mysteries on the Amazon Kindle book Store?

The number of Mystery, Thriller and Suspense eBooks available for sale has grown by 20% over the past year January 2020 to January 2021 and there are about 412, 000 English Kindle titles available across all sub-categories of Mystery, Thriller and Suspense. [Source. K-Lytics Report January 2021]

The good news is that within this large category, there is much less competition in smaller niche subcategories, including Cozy Mysteries.

The amount of competition depends on the number of books available for sale in each niche. The larger the number of books available for readers to purchase, the greater the competition when you launch your book.

Subcategory of Mystery, Thriller and Suspense	Number of eBooks on the Amazon.com store
Mystery-Cozy Overall Subcategory	33,500
Mystery-Cozy Animals	11,000
Mystery-Cozy Culinary	6,000
Mystery-Cozy Crafts and Hobbies	6,000

[Source. K-Lytics Report January 2021. Data rounded to nearest 500.]

Subcategory of Mystery, Thriller and Suspense	Number of eBooks on the Amazon.com store
Mystery-Traditional Detectives	13,500
Mystery-Historical	16,000
Mystery-Private Investigators	21,000
Mystery-Women Sleuths	42,000
Mystery-Amateur Sleuth	8,000
Suspense - Paranormal	24,000
Suspense-Ghosts	3,000
Suspense-Paranormal-Psychics	3,000
Suspense-Paranormal-Werewolves & Shifters	4,000
Suspense-Paranormal-Vampires	4,500

[Source. K-Lytics Report January 2021. Data rounded to nearest 500.]

These subcategories in Mystery, Thriller and Suspense demonstrate that there are many cozy niche markets where there is both low competition and attractive sales rankings on the Amazon Kindle Store.

WHAT IS YOUR NICHE?

How to Research the Market for Your Niche Cozy Mystery

Step One. Take the time to consider where you would want Amazon to place your published book. Which subcategories are the best fit for your work?

Categories make it easier for readers to discover your work, so this is the ideal opportunity to take advantage of these virtual shelves by making sure that the book fits into at least two subcategories.

Many culinary cozy mysteries, for example, also include an animal or pet, so they can be included in both the Culinary and Animals subcategories.

Step Two. Carry our market research on the Kindle Store to determine the current market for your work.

The aim is to research the top Kindle eBooks bestsellers in each of your two main subcategories and collect some statistics about those books.

Whether you are traditionally or independently published, this is where your book will be stacked for readers to browse.

The first thing to do is to determine whether these books are selling. Are readers buying the books you want to write?

Let's take a look at the Amazon.com Kindle store to get an estimate on the number of titles that are available at the time of writing and the subcategories in each niche.

How to Research the Amazon Kindle Market for books with a similar theme to your story idea.

#Go to your Amazon Kindle Store, click on *the Bestsellers and More* option, then scroll down to *Kindle Best Sellers*. Then *Kindle eBooks*.

#Then Select Kindle eBooks on the left sidebar.

This takes you to the main page for all of the categories which are listed on the left side of the page.

#Click on the main category which is the best fit for the kind of book you are looking for and take a look at the options available.

#Choose one subcategory, if there is one, where you know that similar books to yours have been published and scan the bestseller list.

#Open up an Excel spreadsheet or free Google sheet and save it as your working chart. Make a column of numbers from 1 to 50 to get started.

#Starting with the first book on the best sellers list, click on each book, click on the Kindle eBook if there is an option and scroll down to the Product Details for that book.

#Then make a note of the following facts. What is the ranking of the top book, the number 20 book and then number 100 book in that bestselling chart?

The lower the rank, the more popular the book. The bestseller ranking is basically an indication of how many books are selling *better* than yours.

#Follow the thread described above until you find your specific niche.

#Click on the link to that sub-category. You will be shown the top 50 best sellers on the first page and 51 to 100 on the next page.

There is a lot of information here – but right now we are only looking at one thing – the Amazon Kindle eBook or Print book best seller rank.

Example Selected Product details for Witch Is When It All Began (A Witch P.I. Mystery Book 1) by Adele Abbott

- ASIN: B0127HPQ48
- Publisher: Implode Publishing Ltd (August 24, 2015)
- Publication date: August 24, 2015
- Language: English
- Print length: 212 pages.
- Lending : Not Enabled
- Best Sellers Rank: #2,303 in Kindle Store (See Top 100 in Kindle Store)
    - #14 in Witch & Wizard Mysteries
    - #15 in Ghost Mysteries
    - #18 in Cozy Crafts & Hobbies Mystery

What do I look for in these Product Details?

- **The Print Length** which tells me how many pages the print book has, or the number of equivalent pages that Amazon has calculated for this eBook.

- **The Publication Date.** Has this book been recently released?

- **The Sold By details** – has this book been independently published through Amazon, a private publisher name or a traditional publisher.

- **The Amazon Best Sellers Rank** of that book in the subcategories the book is listed in. This is a good indication of how well this book is selling on an hourly basis.

You can also look at the price and whether the book is part of a series, any reviews the book has received and the category listing.

Market Analysis. Worked Example 1. Amazon Cozy Mystery Category Bestsellers

Click on Mystery, Thrillers and Suspense, or the equivalent category on your local Kindle Store, open the category and go to Mystery and then Cozy.

‹ Kindle Store> Kindle eBooks > Mystery, Thriller & Suspense>Mystery>Cozy

Record the Amazon bestseller ranking for books 1 to 20 on your spreadsheet or sheet of paper. Also record the bestseller ranking of the title at position 50 and position 100 – on the next page- in that category.

Reminder – this is a snapshot from one hour in January 2021.

These Amazon charts change rapidly throughout the day, so these results should only be used as examples of the kind of results you could expect.

Here is a summary of the data I have just collected from the bestseller chart for the Cozy Mysteries subcategory on the Amazon.com Kindle store.

General Classification: Top 100 Cozy Mysteries in the US Kindle Chart

Position	Amazon.com Bestseller Ranking	Position	Amazon.com Bestseller Ranking
1	145,187 [anomaly with a mainstream book]	12	989
2	86	13	1,005
3	108	14	1,117
4	355	15	1,202
5	548	16	1,227
6	555	17	1,257
7	584	18	1,297
8	623	19	1,314
9	624	20	1,317
10	827	50	2,344
11	853	100	4,255

Data as of 26 January 2021

Looking at the range of themes in the general Cozy Mystery category, it is clear that:

• the listing includes several mainstream novels which have been assigned to this category because they are probably difficult to fit elsewhere, and they would appeal to readers who enjoy murder mysteries.

There are a lot of historical and literary works listed here plus some hard-boiled crime books which are not a good fit for this category.

• there is an increasing level of crossover into paranormal and supernatural mystery fiction.

Market Analysis. Worked Example 2. Amazon Cozy Mystery Category by Theme.

There are three themes in the Kindle eBook store on Amazon.com:

1. Animals,
2. Crafts and Hobbies and
3. Culinary.

Start by looking at the bestseller Amazon ranking of the top 20 Kindle eBooks in the **Cozy Category in general**. Record the bestseller ranking on your spreadsheet.

Then move down to each of the three sub-categories and repeat the process, making sure that you note down the theme of each book in the bestseller chart.

Amazon Cozy Mysteries by Amazon Kindle Store Ranking for the books in each chart at position 1, 10, 20, 50 and 100.

Chart	#1 Rank	#10 Rank	#20 Rank	#50 Rank	#100 Rank
Animals	335	1,596	2,024	4,349	7,453
Culinary	108	1,317	1,931	4,984	11,425
Crafts and Hobbies	86	1,596	2,361	5,927	12,008

Data as of 26 January 2021

This snapshot exercise indicates that cozy mysteries that have animals on the cover/title/book description and content are overall slightly more popular than Culinary then Crafts and Hobbies cozy mysteries.

But all three groups have excellent sales ranking compared to the rest of the Amazon.com Kindle eBook store which contains millions of books.

Market Analysis. Worked Example 3. Percentage of Paranormal/Supernatural Mysteries compared to percentage of Historical titles in the top 100 Cozy Mysteries.

	% Paranormal	% Mainstream Crime	% Historical
Cozy Overall	21	14	5
Animals	41	4	7
Crafts and Hobbies	49	0	3
Culinary	11	0	6

A quick survey of the 100 titles in each subcategory gives a quick snapshot with a powerful message. – paranormal and supernatural themes are becoming increasingly important to cozy mystery readers.

Market Analysis. Worked Example 4. Amazon.com Bestseller Ranking of Paranormal/Supernatural Niche

If your book has a paranormal or supernatural theme, follow the same process but click on the Suspense Category under Mystery, Thriller and Suspense and follow the link to the Paranormal sub-category.

‹ Kindle eBooks
- ‹ Mystery, Thriller & Suspense
  - ‹ Suspense
    - Paranormal
      - Psychics
      - Vampires
      - Werewolves & Shifters

In addition, you will also see paranormal mystery eBooks listed in the print book category for Mystery-Supernatural.

‹ Books
- ‹ Mystery, Thriller & Suspense
  - ‹ Mystery
    - Supernatural
      - Ghosts
      - Psychics
      - Vampires
      - Werewolves & Shifters
      - **Witches & Wizards**

Don't worry that this category is for supernatural print books. You will find that most of the books listed are Kindle Edition format.

Comparison of Paranormal Themes by Bestseller Ranking on Amazon.com

Chart	#1 Rank	#10 Rank	#20 Rank	#50 Rank	#100 Rank
Supernatural	340	1,264	2,069	3,625	4,833
Ghosts	827	2,163	3,844	6,442	7,768
Witches and Wizards	340	2,163	3,604	6,707	11,123
Werewolves/ Shifters	201	763	1,440	3,117	7,931
Psychics	1,640	3,268	4,451	7,664	13,286
Vampires	52	1,045	2,047	4,711	10,203

Data as of 26 January 2021

Next Question – Are these mystery Kindle books selling?

Amazon.com Kindle Bestseller Rank	Estimated Sales per day
300	333
500	175
700	131
1,000	113
2,000	90
3,000	70
4,000	52
6,000	24
8,000	19
10,000	15
20,000	13

https://kindlepreneur.com/amazon-kdp-sales-rank-calculator/

The answer is a definite yes, cozy mystery and supernatural mystery Kindle eBooks are extremely popular in all the subcategories on the Kindle store and there is huge potential for growth.

Summary.

I hope that these market reviews have demonstrated how much free market information is available on the Amazon.com Kindle store and how you can use the bestseller rankings to determine the size of the market for the theme and ideal niche category for your project.

These numbers will be constantly changing so it is always useful to check:

- the size of your potential market in a specific subcategory

- the size of the potential competition with other mystery series which use the same theme and niche.

For me, the data clearly demonstrates the need to use the secondary subcategories whenever you can to help direct readers to the specific theme or themes of your murder mystery.

If you have the opportunity to include an animal, for instance, or a paranormal thread into your story then it could be a fun experiment.

Make it as easy as possible for readers to find your books. Think niche and think theme. Then enjoy the writing, knowing that there is an audience for the books you love to read and write.

THE IDEAL WORDCOUNT FOR MODERN COZY MYSTERIES

Any fiction writer will tell you that a book has a natural length. It will contain as many pages as are needed to tell the story in the best way possible.

Absolutely correct.

If you love to read and want to write short novels, perhaps 40,000 to 60,000 words in length, that's fantastic. Readers will enjoy spending time with your characters for a few hours.

On the other hand, there are many mystery writers who feel that their murder can only be solved in a full-length novel, which normally contains between 65,000 to 90,000 words. Their readers dive into the expanded story world and get to know the cast of characters in depth. There may be more murders, a wider range of suspects and many more subplots for readers to enjoy.

I like to think of short novels as individual episodes in a long-running crime series, whereas a full-length novel is the equivalent of a two-hour movie in the cinema.

Both are complete stories with a start, middle and end, with characters to care about, but they serve different audiences with different needs.

These are very general guidelines and wordcount varies enormously depending on the genre of your work.

Which is why it is imperative that you understand the market for both shorter Kindle cozy mysteries and longer books.

It can also help you to consider the best publishing model for your specific book.

How does Amazon calculate the page length of a Kindle eBook?

If there is a print format of the eBook, then Amazon will use the same page count as the print edition so as to avoid confusion. It should be noted that the eBook page may not be a perfect match to the page number in the print book.

If there is not a print edition, Amazon will calculate a page count based on standard settings.

Amazon KDP states: "The estimated length is calculated using the number of page turns on a Kindle using settings to closely represent a physical book."

This corresponds to the following Kindle settings:

Font size: smallest

Typeface: condensed

Line Spacing: small

Words per Line: default.

The results will therefore be different depending on which Kindle device or app you are using, but these settings are equivalent to approximately 250-300 words per page on average.

Market Analysis Exercise.

Worked Example 5. Amazon Cozy Mysteries by Page Count

The product details for each book contains the page count, or equivalent electronic page count, of that book. I have reviewed the page count for the **Top 100 Kindle Cozy Bestsellers (excluding box sets and short stories)** by Best Seller Rank on Amazon.com. All data as on 26th January 2021.

The Average Page count for the top 100 Cozy eBooks = 261 pages

If we take the average page count to be around 250 words per printed page this equates to an average book length of approx. 65,000 words.

But there is a lot more detail underneath that average number.

Let's sort the results into three groups according to publisher.

Group One. Independent publishers.

The Average Page Count of Independently published books = 224 pages.

If we take the average page count to be around 250 words per printed page this equates to an average book length of approx. 56,000 words.

40% of the top 100 Cozy Mysteries were independently published books.

Group Two. All traditional publishers.

The Average Page Count of Traditionally published books = 289 pages

This group includes: Amazon Lake Union, Amazon Thomas and Mercer, Joffe, Kensington, Penguin, Atlantic, Boldwood, Bookouture and Crooked Lane at the time of review, but this of course subject to change with new books being released every day by numerous traditional publishing lines.

If we take the average page count to be around 250 words per printed page this equates to an average book length of approx. 72,000 words.

Group Three. Kensington Books

The Average Page Count of books published by Kensington = 319 pages

It is very clear that this analysis that traditional publishers, and especially an established publisher such as Kensington Books, are releasing much longer books compared to independently published authors.

The average page length of 319 pages is skewed towards longer length books. If we take the average page count to be around 250 words per printed page this equates to an average book length of approx. 80,000 words.

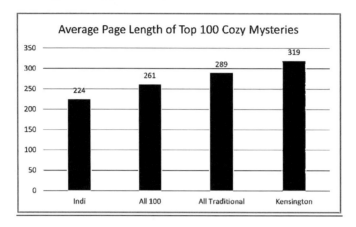

This is consistent with the submission guidelines of these publishers who would normally be looking for manuscripts for full-length novels of at least 70,000 to 75,000 words.

In contrast, independent authors are creating shorter novels. The average page length of 224 pages, or 56,000 words at 250 words a page, is skewed towards shorter books. In fact, many independently published books are much shorter.

For example. The popular author Kathi Daley has two titles in the top 100 cozy mystery category with page counts of 125 and 133 – both less than 40,000 words.

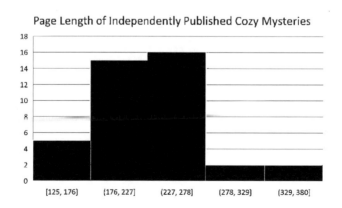

How to select the best publishing model for your work

The implications are clear. Once you have carried out this market analysis and identified books that are a good match to the mystery that you would love to write, then you need to consider carefully how you can share your work in the most effective way possible.

If you prefer to write full-length fiction of 70,000 words or more, then you should consider approaching a literary agent and/or submitting directly to a traditional publisher if they accept un-agented submissions.

Submission Guidelines for Cozy Mystery Publishers

You can find the submission guidelines of the traditional publishers on their company websites.

Agent Submission Only Publishers

Amazon Lake Union and Amazon Thomas and Mercer are agent only.

Berkley is an imprint of Penguin Publishing and agent only.

Open Road Media is agent only.

Mysterious Press are not currently open to submissions for new fiction and are agent only.

Minotaur Books is an imprint of St. Martin's Press/ PanMacmillan and agent only.

William Morrow is an imprint of HarperCollins and agent only.

Publishers who do accept Unsolicited Submissions.

Crooked Lane Books do accept submissions from authors.

Kensington books do accept submissions from authors.

Joffe Books do accept submissions from authors.

This is only a small sample, since the publishing world is slowly adapting to digital distribution, and many traditional publishers are introducing commercial genre fiction lines, including crime and mystery novels. Keep browsing the bestseller charts and take note of unfamiliar new publishers who could be the perfect partner for your unique book.

Why traditional publishing is not the best publishing model for all cozy mysteries.

Bottom line. Publishing houses are businesses and books are "products".

Authors create the products which publishers have to edit, design, curate, print/publish worldwide and then sell to a dwindling number of bookstores and libraries etc. Their job is to make a return on this significant investment in time and money so that the business can remain profitable.

I am sorry if that offends those of an artistic temperament, but publishers don't owe authors a living.

They are loyal to their authors and do their best in difficult market conditions, but if your first and second books do not sell, then an editor can find it hard to persuade the marketing team to commit to taking more. This is a market driven business.

No profit, no business. Same the world over. The challenge is that they have to make a profit with books at a price point which is commercially viable.

How this impacts the books we are writing.

Consider it this way.

If you were pitching your work to the equivalent of a venture capitalist like a literary agent or submission editor, how would you do it? What would you say?

"I am going to work for months and invest hundreds of pounds/dollars to create a series of books which I plan to sell online for 99 cents."

You would expect them to ask sensible questions such as:

- How many copies are you going to sell in a short time?
- What is your marketing plan?
- What is your current social media following under your author brand? How do you plan to reach your ideal readers?

In other words – how can I get a return on my investment of time and money in your work.

My answers?

- My price point is 99 cents because that is the market price for debut short cozy mysteries for a new author in this cozy niche with online book retailers.
- I don't know how many copies I will sell.
- Yes, I have a marketing plan and it is rolling out over the next few weeks.
- Right now. I am launching a brand-new author brand, so I don't have a social media following for my new pen name.

Yes, I have a track record as a writer, so they know that I can string words together in joined up writing. But this is a new genre. New brand. New audience. New market. Crazy low price.

Will these books make a profit? Long term I sincerely hope so. But short term? I am willing to take that risk and invest my time and huge amounts of energy in a new cozy mystery series.

Would I be surprised if literary agents and publishers were not keen to do the same from a business point of view? Perhaps not.

The Middle way. Digital First Publishers

As well as traditional publishers, there are numerous digital-first publishers who will take over the editing and publishing side of the business while you handle the writing – but you will still have to do a lot of the marketing and launch activities. Most of these companies release the eBook and the print on demand paperback to online publishing platforms and have a marketing budget, but some are eBook only, so you should always check the details of the offer.

Most digital-first contracts don't offer an advance on royalties when you sign the contract, but instead provide a much higher royalty per sale, which can be up to 50% of the net eBook income. The publisher has a lower investment and consequently lower risk. The book may sell at a lower price, but this can quickly translate to a greater number of sales given a real marketing push. And with a higher royalty payment, the author sees the financial benefit immediately.

One big advantage of digital-first publishing is the faster lead-time, with changes possible until quite close to publication. Traditionally published books can take 18 months to get into print after the manuscript has been accepted. Digital first books can be released in months.

Digital-first companies who are interested in mystery fiction include the following, but there are many other options available:

Bookouture, is open to submissions for full length fiction of 70,000 words plus when I last checked.

HQDigital, is open to submissions and prefers manuscripts of 60,000 words plus.

Beyond the Page Publishing is open to submissions.

Canelo Books (not accepting unsolicited submissions at this time but this is subject to change.)

You should always look carefully at their book covers, author royalty rates, book marketing plans, the sales ranking of the books they publish and the authors who have opted to place their work with them.

Righty. At this point you should have a much better understanding of the potential market for the specific type of mystery that you want to write.

Let's move on to the fun part. Writing the book!

THE THREE HOOKS AND A SLEUTH STORY GENERATOR

THE THREE HOOKS AND A SLEUTH STORY GENERATOR

Every author is different. Many start a new story with a vague idea that they want to explore. Some have an intriguing character that demands to have their story told, while others want to work on a particular setting or find out how a murder method could be used.

Your story. Your process.

One thing however is true for all of us. It is essential that we test out whether our story idea is strong enough to support an entire novel, **before we write it**.

I am not talking about building a synopsis or outline. That will come much later.

The goal is to work with a nebulous vague concept for a mystery novel and develop and expand that concept into a strong and totally cool idea that will be a delight to write – and will instantly grab the attention of your ideal audience.

THE HIGH CONCEPT STORY IDEA

What is high concept and why is it so important for ideas to be high concept?

You may have heard of the term "high-concept premise" or "elevator pitch".

This is a one sentence description of your story idea that encapsulates the entire story in a simple way that is easy to someone to understand and immediately tells the reader why this story is unique, fresh, and intriguing.

Why "high-concept"? Because the author has worked hard to find something new, cool, and interesting about their story idea that has not been read hundreds of times before. They have added a unique twist or blended genres and ideas to create something different.

It is the magical factor that will make your book irresistible to both readers and potential agents and publishers.

"High concept ideas tend to stick in a person's mind," says Danielle Burby, an agent at Nelson Literary Agency. "High concept is all about big ideas, high stakes, and clear communication."

Here are a few examples of well-known high-concept novels:

- An eleven-year-old boy discovers he's a wizard and that a notorious wizard murdered his parents. (The Harry Potter series)
- In a dystopian society, teenagers are randomly selected from each district to fight to the death on television. (The Hunger Games series)
- A bored and miserable meteorologist is stuck living the same day over and over. (*Groundhog Day*)

The character in these stories is not so unique – but then the author takes each of these ideas and combines them with an interesting concept and raises the stakes by asking, "**What if**?"

Consider your own buying patterns.

When you read the online book description for any cozy mystery, the plot will be summarized into a few short paragraphs which have been carefully written to attract the ideal reader and intrigue them enough to buy the book or look inside the sample to find out more.

In effect, your book description is the sales and marketing tool for that book. A reader will look at your book then read the book details.

So, what makes a book irresistible to cozy mystery readers?

- What would make you instantly click the buy button or put the print book in your basket in the bookstore?
- What would get you interested and excited about a book?

- And, if you are pitching that book to a literary agent or editor at a publishing house, what would make them invest time reading your book proposal?

How is that even possible? Surely every variation of a cozy mystery has already been done before? How can I come up with something new in this genre?

Answer? You spend the time pre-writing to transform your initial idea into a new and irresistible story idea that promises to deliver a specific kind of emotional journey for your reader.

So, how do you come up with your magical high-concept story idea?

Creativity is your superpower. Now it is time to put that creativity to work.

There are four key elements I am looking for in the description of any cozy mystery. I call this: **The Three Hooks and a Sleuth Story Generator.**

What exactly is a Story Hook?

For me, a story hook is something that grabs a reader's attention, immediately creates questions that demand to be answered and makes someone want to read this book or watch the TV show or movie.

It could be something cool, different or interesting or intriguing, but it has to be attention grabbing.

Think of the headlines in an online blog post or newspaper. They are called "click-bait" for a reason!

Hooks are context specific and apply to different genres and audiences.

One top tip is to imagine what the movie poster for your book would look like. Think about the banner headline for your book that is splashed across this poster. What sentence would you use to describe the book and make it irresistible?

You can find examples of these hooks on movie posters, TV trailers and in your local online or print TV listings.

Here are a few random examples from popular movies and TV shows.

White Collar. **What if?** A white-collar criminal agrees to help the FBI catch other white-collar criminals using his expertise as an art and securities thief, counterfeiter, and conman.

Murder Mystery (Netflix). **What if?** On a long-awaited trip to Europe, a New York City cop and his hairdresser wife scramble to solve a baffling murder aboard a billionaire's yacht.

Big Little Lies. **What if?** The apparently perfect lives of upper-class mothers, at a prestigious elementary school, unravel to the point of murder when a single mother moves to their quaint Californian beach town.

 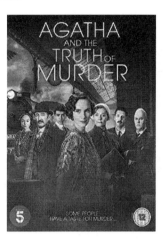

KNIVES OUT. HELL, ANY OF THEM COULD HAVE DONE IT. **What if?** A detective investigates the death of a patriarch of an eccentric, combative family.

AGATHA AND THE TRUTH OF MURDER. SOME PEOPLE HAVE A TASTE FOR MURDER. **What if?** In 1926, with her writing in crisis and her personal life in tatters, a young Agatha Christie decides to solve a real-life murder.

How to Develop High-Concept Cozy Mystery Book Ideas

After reading hundreds of cozy mysteries and watching countless movies and TV series, I believe that the key story hooks for cozy mysteries fall into four types.

THE THREE HOOKS AND A SLEUTH STORY GENERATOR

Hook 1. Who is your sleuth and how does the sleuth become involved in the murder investigation?

The goal of a murder mystery is to solve the puzzle of the murder and identify the killer, and the sleuth has to become brave and take risks to survive.

Hook 2. How is this different, intriguing and new in some way? Can you create a great high-concept story idea?

What is different about your story idea that makes it sound cool, interesting, and fresh? Yes, readers are looking for similar elements within a specific niche but are quickly bored with copycat story ideas. Channel your creativity. Come up with a fresh twist.

Hook 3. What is the theme of the book? This instantly tells the reader exactly what kind of book they should expect.

For example: animals, culinary, historical, paranormal, crafts and hobbies, private investigators, amateur sleuths, small town, and many others.

The theme acts as a shortcut into the story for the reader, supported by the book cover design and book description, but you do have to deliver on that promise.

Hook 4. What emotional experience does this book promise to deliver?

What is the tone of the book? How do I feel when I read the book description? What kind of emotional buttons does this book idea press? Popular topics include personal re-invention after loss or betrayal, winning against injustice and restoring balance to a fractured community.

There could be a few scary moments, but overall, your story idea should take the reader on a positive and escapist emotional journey away from their everyday lives. Readers are looking for charm and nostalgia. There is a reason why these books are called "Cozy" mysteries.

Let's dive deeper into some recent examples to understand what makes these story hooks so attractive and how the four-hook story generator works in practice.

Enola Holmes (2020)

Movie Description for the film adaptation of the book.

While searching for her missing mother, intrepid teen Enola Holmes uses her sleuthing skills to outsmart big brother Sherlock and help a runaway lord.

Hook 1. Who is the sleuth and how does the sleuth become involved in the murder investigation?

Enola Holmes is a teenager who sets out to find her missing mother.

Hook 2. How is this different, intriguing and new is some way?

Enola is the teenage sister of Sherlock Holmes and yet she is going to become a super-sleuth and outwit her famous brother and solve a dangerous conspiracy.

Hook 3. What is the theme of the book?

Sherlock Holmes stories are set in Victorian or Edwardian England, so this is an historical mystery.

Hook 4. What emotional experience does this story promise to deliver?

Fun, light-hearted adventure and coming of age experience with a positive escapist feel, including a sweet teen romance subplot.

Three Hooks and a Sleuth: Example 1. The Inn at Holiday Bay: Proof in the Photo by Kathi Daley

Hook 1. Who is the sleuth? What do they do and why are they in this murder mystery? Abby Sullivan owns a seaside mansion, the Holiday Inn.

Hook 2. How does the sleuth get involved in the murder investigation? A guest at the inn is murdered.

Hook 3. What are the two main themes of the book? Animals and Cozy Culinary Mystery. Abby adopts a cat and a dog.

Hook 4. What emotional experience does this book promise to deliver? "A heart-warming cozy mystery series about losing everything, taking a chance, and starting again."

Three Hooks and a Sleuth: Example 2: Kitty Confidential (Pet Whisperer P.I. Book 1) by Molly Fitz

Hook 1. Who is the sleuth? What do they do and why are they in this murder mystery? A 27-year-old paralegal in Blueberry Bay law firm.

Hook 2. How does the sleuth get involved in the murder investigation? She is electrocuted by a faulty coffee maker and wakes up a cat whisperer, and the cat tells her that his owner was killed.

Hook 3. What are the two main themes of the book? Cozy Animal and Amateur Sleuth. The sleuth can talk to animals, starting with a cat.

Hook 4. What emotional experience does this book promise to deliver? Fun, fast paced, escapist read with a talking cat who helps solve the murder.

Three Hooks and a Sleuth: Example 3: The Vampire Knitting Club: First in a Paranormal Cozy Mystery Series by Nancy Warren

Hook 1. Who is the sleuth? What do they do and why are they in this murder mystery? Lucy Swift has come to Oxford to visit her grandmother.

Hook 2. How does the sleuth get involved in the murder investigation? She finds out that her much-loved grandmother was murdered and turned into a vampire.

Hook 3. What are the two main themes of the book? Supernatural Vampire Mystery and Cozy Craft and Hobby. Lucy has inherited a knitting shop and a resident collection of vampires who live in her basement, and there is a hint that she could be a witch. Lucy does also inherit a cat, but this is not a key theme.

This is a really different and cool high concept combination of knitting shop and vampires.

Hook 4. What emotional experience does this book promise to deliver?

Emotional, very different, escapist read set in a knitting shop with a talking murder victim, so the reader can expect paranormal twists and story points. This combination is intriguing - I would want to find out more.

Here are a few more examples to demonstrate the versatility of this technique.

All of the following worked examples are story ideas that I am working on or have personally worked on in the past.

Worked Example. Susie Sleuth

Hook 1. Who is the sleuth? What do they do?
What if? Susie Sleuth is a widowed schoolteacher in the small rocky mountain town she moved to as a teenager 50 years ago.
How does the sleuth get involved in the murder investigation?
What if? Susie finds the dead body of her best friend's cheating and soon to be ex-husband stretched out on her kitchen floor with her dog licking his face.
Hook 2. How is this different and new is some way?
What if? Susie's husband was the local police chief in this small mountain town, and she knows everyone he ever arrested. Now she is going to pull together a top team of quirky local criminals to find out who did this before her friend is arrested. [fun idea with ex-con investigations].   AND/OR   What if? Her best friend moved to the town as part of witness protection because her husband was a professional assassin working for a drug lord in the city. Have they finally tracked him down to this small town? Or is the killer closer to home? [fun idea around witness protection in small towns]
Hook 3. What are the two main themes of the book?
Animals. Crafts and Hobbies.
Hook 4. What emotional experience does this book promise to deliver?
Cozy mountain village with fun characters who have known one another for decades.

Worked Example. Amy Sleuth

Hook 1. Who is the sleuth? What do they do?
What if? Amy Sleuth is an office worker in her twenties in a London suburb who spends her Friday evenings at the craft club her aunt runs at a local cafe.
How does the sleuth get involved in the murder investigation?
What if? Amy arrives early for the weekly club meeting and finds one of the members has been murdered with a strange knitting needle.
Hook 2. How is this different and new is some way?
What if? Amy's aunt secretly belongs to a group of psychics with attitude and the murder weapon is a vintage wand belonging to her aunt.
What if? The victim was a psychic who had been working with the parents of a missing man. She had arranged to see the family after the knitting club because she had new important information to share. When Amy touched the victim as she lay dying, she took on all of the psychic's amazing abilities, including her visions of the missing person, putting her life in danger.
Hook 3. What are the two main themes of the book?
Crafts and Hobbies. Supernatural Witches and Psychics.
Hook 4. What emotional experience does this book promise to deliver?
Warm and cozy knitting and craft details and fun collection of elderly psychics with attitude.
What happens when you suddenly have psychic powers you did not want or expect. How do you handle that?

From these brief examples, you can see that the opportunities are endless!

You can create any kind of sleuth your imagination and creativity can come up with and then place them in the wrong place at the wrong time.

Then ask the tough questions.

Does your new story idea sound intriguing? Would you like to find out more?

If the answer is yes, now is the time to develop your story idea so that these four elements feel exciting and interesting to the point where you cannot wait to start writing the story.

Still not working? Put that idea to one side and move on to another idea.

My suggestion is to use this technique to kick start your imagination to come up with multiple options and story ideas.

Don't worry if this all feels a bit unfocused.

In this step we are still very much in the story development stage and your idea could, and probably will, change and move into other directions the second you start writing and the characters develop inside the story world you create for them.

This is why this high-level technique can be used by both plotters and pantsers.

By staying open to new ideas, you allow your creativity and imagination to explore the full potential of the idea and test out where it will take you.

This is the fun time!

Now it is time to expand on ONE of those story ideas and see where it takes you.

Save the ones you don't use – you may well come back to them for another series.

Go back to your notebook and quickly expand on your notes for one of the story scenarios.

EXPAND THE ONE LINE STORY IDEA INTO A PREMISE FOR YOUR MYSTERY

This is where you move from the general and vague to the specific.

You expand the basic concept into a few sentences and add characters, settings, murders and victims, plots, and subplots.

The good news is that if you work on this basic overall summary now, you can save a lot of time, energy, and heartbreak in the future.

It is much better to find out now before you invest weeks of time and frustration and energy writing a story that fails to take off, does not light your creative fire or simply runs out of steam.

Challenge your story and work on any weak threads or plot lines.

Remember. These are your notes for the first draft.

Nobody else will see them unless you want to share them with friends and your editor or literary agent.

The whole story is not described – just the essential aspects of the key events in the opening chapters.

By the time you reach the end of your first draft of the manuscript, the story will have developed and shifted away from the original summary.

This is completely normal and should be expected to happen.

The good news is that you can use the Three Hooks and a Sleuth Story Generator technique to rapidly kick-start the story development process for your book and then build the working outline for your manuscript.

STORY IDEA CHECKLIST FOR A COZY MURDER MYSTERY

Premise checklist for a murder mystery:

1. Your compelling sleuth as the main character.
2. The ordinary life of the sleuth and why they are having personal problems at the start of the story before the inciting incident. This is the start of their character arc.
3. The incident which compels them to investigate this murder and discover who took this person's life. They must have a compelling reason to investigate this murder. They need to be driven to find the killer. Not just out of curious interest.
4. What makes this sleuth and the story situation different and fresh and intriguing. Does it pass the high-concept test?
5. The bigger opposition the sleuth will face as they investigate.
6. You have an interesting location and time period to stage your murder investigation.
7. The reader can instantly see what themes you are using as a quick insight into the kind of story they expect to read.

PRE-WRITING EXERCISES

Quickly grab your notebook and write down at least four, and preferably more, different new ideas for a cozy mystery using the Four Hooks technique.

Step One. Play the What If game using Hook 1.

Who is your sleuth and how does the sleuth become involved in the murder investigation?

Worked Example. Emilia Sleuth

Hook 1. Who is the sleuth? What do they do and why are they in this murder mystery?
What if? Emilia Sleuth is a young widow in the 1930s, sailing from London to New York on a luxury passenger liner.
How does the sleuth get involved in the murder investigation?
What if? Emilia makes friends with another single lady in the first-class section on the ship and becomes a suspect when this lady is found murdered in her cabin.

Step Two. Play the What If game using Hook 2.

How is this Story Different in some Way?

Hook 2. How is this different and new is some way?
What if? **Emilia is actually a lady Pinkerton Detective Agent** working undercover on the ship. She was investigating the victim but is sworn to secrecy. But what was the victim hiding that was so important that she had to be silenced? And who killed her? More importantly, the killer is still on the ship. Is Emily in danger?

What if? The victim is the beautiful but flighty society daughter of a New York banker who is travelling with her chaperone. She has been recalled home from finishing school after she was involved in a scandalous affair with the handsome and educated Maharajah of Kalapur. But then the fabulous Kalapur rubies are reported missing. Are they on the ship? And can Emily find the killer before the reach New York?

Step Three. Add in some ideas for Hooks 3 and 4 for this story idea.

Hook 3. What are the main themes of the book?
Historical. Private Investigators. Women sleuths. Women's fiction. Traditional Detectives.
Hook 4. What emotional experience does this book promise to deliver?
Historical mystery set in fascinating inter-war period with reference to class and social structures and the lifestyle of the wealthy. (Downton Abbey at sea.)

You can see that there are multiple storylines that spin out from this scenario. A lady Pinkerton agent could be sent on new cases that could be used to create an entire series of books with Emilia Sleuth.

If you can build in the potential to write a series of linked books featuring the same main character, this will definitely increase your chance of being a commercial success, irrespective of whether you are independently publishing your work or pitching the story to an agent or editor.

I hope that you can see that once you have this approach you can quickly turn the spark of an idea into four hooks.

FOUR ACT STORY STRUCTURE

HOW TO USE STORY STRUCTURE

Story Structure for Intuitive Writers

I know that many authors are intuitive writers who hate the idea of outlining their novel before diving into the writing. They worry that they will lose the magical spark of discovery that emerges when they get their characters on the page inside the story world.

If that is your process and it works for you, great!

You can use the three hooks and a sleuth story generator to come up with a great idea for your story – then start working on the text!

Most authors use the momentum and energy that comes from diving into a new idea to power them to the end of the story. This "discovery" draft is the working first draft of your mystery.

It is at this point that you can get to work and use story structure to shape your work into the most effective form possible for readers.

Yes, it may mean cutting and adding scenes and dialogue, but the end result will be a second draft which delivers the emotional experience you want to create.

The Power of Story Structure

Whether you use story structure to create an outline for your mystery as part of your pre-writing process, or come to it after creating your first draft, the process is exactly the same.

You are breaking your story down into a story pattern that readers of this genre will recognise.

What do I mean by that? Modern readers expect to be entertained.

In a cozy mystery you have made a promise to your reader that the sleuth is going to solve a crime by the end of the book.

In the process, you will take your readers on an emotional roller coaster of a journey with the sleuth – and the stages of that journey are very specific to cozy mystery fiction.

Story Structure Patterns

There are certain storytelling conventions which have become engrained into our minds through every book that we have ever read, and every play, radio drama, TV show or movie that we have ever seen, from animated cartoons to the latest action-packed blockbuster of a thriller.

You may not even be aware of these subconscious expectations because they are totally enmeshed in our brains, but as readers we expect the story to be developed in a certain pattern and sequence of events and revelations and stages. All the reader cares about is the emotional experience that you have created for them on the page.

Now is the time to start working on the story structure of that working draft so that you can take your sleuth on an emotional journey as they investigate the murder or murders, which demonstrates the full potential of your characters and the story situation that you have created.

The best analysis of story structure comes from screenwriters. Their job is to choreograph the emotions of the audience who is watching the movie.

So, what are these story structure patterns?

How are stories really structured, and how can you use them to build the optimal structure for your story?

I've spent years studying the best storytelling teachers, including Joseph Campbell, Robert McKee, John Truby, Blake Synder and Christopher Vogler.

Plus, as a published author with Mills and Boon and HarperCollins, I have worked with several brilliant editors who have shared with me in-depth information about story structure, character development and how to write compelling fiction.

I learnt how to combine story craft with genre specific story structure to create award-winning fiction.

In this part of the book, I am going to share with you some of the deep story structure craft that I have learnt as a full-time writer.

And more importantly, how you can use that story structure to take YOUR story from good to great.

Please note that I make no apologies for the fact that I am a scientist so there may be tables, charts, and lists.

That is how my scientist brain works but it may not be your process and that's totally cool. These ideas are not designed to intimidate you. Far from it.

My goal is to give you a solid framework for any cozy mystery you can adapt, use, take which parts make sense and then apply it to your outline or draft.

Imagine that you are building a house.

You start at the bottom with the foundations, the groundwork, the floor layout, and underpinnings of the structure. Then the building work begins for an office block, residential home, or a retail store – whatever your plan dictates.

Story structure is the equivalent foundations which underpin all of your work.

On top of those foundations, you can build any kind of fresh and new story you like, of any length and in any genre. The foundations of the story stay the same.

The story you build on those foundations is your creative genius - but you need that solid structural framework to support the weight of your story.

Does that make sense? I hope so.

Screenwriting Techniques and Fiction

The good news is that the same story structure techniques used by screenwriters can be applied to fiction. And especially commercial genre fiction.

I believe that the best model for commercial genre fiction is Four Act story structure.

Why? Because the goal of a screenwriter is precisely the same as a novelist – to create a compelling emotional journey for the audience/readers, and there can be no better journey than the up and down rollercoaster ride of crime fiction.

Classical Four Act Story Structure

In a properly structured movie or novel, the story consists of Four Acts, which are defined by nine key plot points. Not only are these plot points always the same; they usually occupy the same positions in the story.

This means that your first draft of the novel needs to have a number of key dramatic twists, sudden obstacles or reveals, called **"turning points"**, when the story shifts in some remarkable way, or something is revealed, action must be taken, and the stakes increase.

Scenes, Sequences and Four Acts

In classical story structure, scenes are collected into Sequences of scenes where **there is a start, middle and end to each Scene Sequence.**

- **Every scene ends with a turning point that hooks onto the next scene.**
- **Every Sequence ends with a bigger turning point that hooks onto the next Scene Sequence.**
- **Sequences of scenes are then collected together to form Acts.**
- **Every Act ends with a major turning point that hooks onto the first scene of the next Sequence of the next Act.**

In this way, the story moves on and builds, and instead of a sagging middle, the emotional and story tension builds at a controlled pace that will have the readers turning the page to find out what happens next.

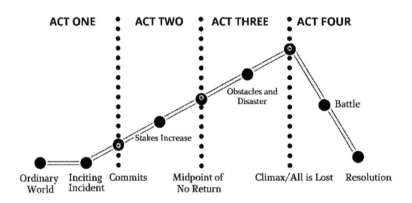

In this way, the story moves on and builds and each scene, Sequence of scenes and Act pivots into the next unit of action and there are no sagging middles.

What's more, the twist at the end of every scene, scene Sequence and then Act, makes sure that the tension and conflict is always building, keeping the story moving and the reader totally hooked on your story.

You are totally in control over how you create a page-turning read!

Clearly the number of scenes in each Sequence will depend on the length of your work. If you are writing a long novel, there could be three or four Sequences of scenes per Act, broken into chapters, while a short story may only have one scene for each of the four Acts.

For most genre fiction novels, there could be two or three short scenes in a Sequence and each chapter is a Sequence.

For very fast paced mystery novels, each chapter may contain only one long scene. It is entirely up to you!

MURDER MYSTERY STORY STRUCTURE

Any cozy mystery book has obligatory scenes and a recognisable story structure, just as any other form of genre fiction.

Readers expect to see a traditional pattern of events, clues and reveals, setbacks and dead ends, leading to a climax final confrontation between the sleuth and the real killer.

I start by breaking the storyline down into 4 Acts.

Then each of the 4 Acts has 4 sequences of scenes, so I start with an outline broken down into 16 sequences.

ACT ONE: SEQUENCES 1 TO 4

ACT TWO: SEQUENCES 5 TO 8

ACT THREE: SEQUENCES 9 TO 12

ACT FOUR: SEQUENCES 13 TO 16.

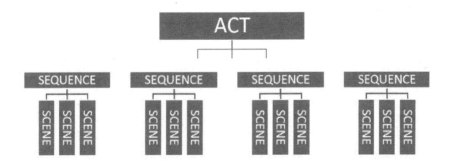

I can move these 16 Sequences around to create the most compelling version of my story for the reader. I may not need 16 Sequences of scenes, or I might need to add more steps, but it is somewhere to start.

By the end of the project, I know that this could completely change, but this simple outline is the key to building an effective working first draft of the story.

In the following section, I will share with you a simple template story structure for a cozy mystery novel of any length.

This is what I feel should be in each Sequence of scenes for the mystery plot to work.

I see these elements as signposts that take the reader from the start to the end of the murder mystery journey.

Important. My personal story structure map is not a formula, or join-the-dots writing, but rather a story pattern that I think cozy mystery readers (like myself) will recognise and enjoy.

This works for me, but it may not be a good fit for your project or your writing process. Go with whatever works for you!

It can also be used as an editing tool for intuitive writers when they have completed the first draft.

COZY MYSTERY PLOT TEMPLATE

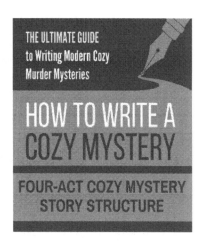

My Combined Story Plan for a Four-Act Cozy Mystery with 16 Sequences of Scenes

ACT ONE

ACT ONE is made up of 4 Sequences of Scenes:

Sequence 1. Characters and world building.

Sequence 2. Conflict and the Inciting Incident.

Sequence 3. Reaction to the Crime or Incident.

Sequence 4. Commitment to Finding the Killer.

The opening sequences of scenes have to do a lot of heavy lifting.
Since this is my first draft, I am not worried about making each word perfect.

This is getting the story down and the characters onto the page, acting and reacting and revealing more about themselves.
By the end of Act One, I should have clear signposts about where this story is going and how I am going to get there.

Sequence 1. Characters and World Building.

Introduce the main characters in their story worlds and situations.

The opening pages establish who the main character is and what the main character's internal and external problems are. It also establishes the setting, period, tone, style, and point of view of the story.

#In most cases I would recommend introducing your sleuth to the reader as soon as possible since they are the main character the reader will be following in this story. They have to understand who this character is and what his or her world looks like.

Note: I am using an example of a female sleuth as a working example, but the same principles apply for any gender or creature.

Let the reader know in the first scene/first chapter who the main character is and why they should care what happens to them.

Show that she is skilled and has talents and strengths and can handle herself.

#This is the Start of the Personal line for the detective as well as an Action line in this story.

Introducing the internal conflict of the sleuth at this point builds to a double resolution for both the personal line of the character and the plot line at the end.

Perfect people living perfect lives are not only boring but not credible as living and breathing people.

- **Who is the sleuth?**
- **What is the sleuth ultimately looking for?**
- **What is missing in the sleuth's own life?**
- **Is the sleuth likeable? Do you want to spend time reading about this person and sharing their life for the hours it takes to enjoy the book?**
- **Can the reader recognise themselves in this character and relate to them?**

Everyone is facing challenges in their ordinary lives and your sleuth should be no different.

The problem could be physical, emotional, psychological or any combination of the three, but there has to be something that they need rather than want, even if they don't realise it.

Perhaps they are dealing with loss, illness, money problems or it could be that one or both parents, or parent figures, are absent in their life or critical of their decisions?

This is the person the reader wants to be with the whole way through the story so there has to be some empathy/sympathy for them at the start- the audience has to care about them.

TOP TIP. Let the sleuth show some compassion, generosity and kindness for another person or animal or the natural world. That compassion and understanding will shine through as a strength.

You need this type of strength to balance out their stubborn resolve and determination to walk into dangerous situations on their own later in the book.

Don't feel that you don't need to cram all of his or her special talents into the opening chapters, together with a full biography since their first birthday.

Far from it. It is better to reveal these strengths and weave in the backstory as the sleuth reacts to the actions of the killer and the ups and downs of the murder investigation.

Hook. What makes this person cool, interesting and different?

This is linked to the theme of your cozy mystery. Culinary, hobbies and crafts, animals or paranormal. What makes this character different? What special skills, talents and abilities does she have as a result of this theme?

Hook the reader in the first paragraph by hinting at a turning point or crisis in her life.

[Handwritten at top: French: librarian, tour guide, she lost a job at a museum... (concierge?) Chef, maid?]

Give the reader some reason to root for this character. Why are they at the end of their tether when the story begins?

For example, they may have just lost their job, their business is in financial danger or their personal relationships are a disaster.

Who are the levels of detective?

- Who are her friends and family and the people she would rather avoid if she could?
- Who is the sidekick or sidekicks our sleuth is going to talk to and hash things out with?
- Are there enforcement authorities and family members?

They should have the skills that the sleuth does not have, plus humour and quirky characteristics or even add a bit of conflict into the investigation.

TOP TIP. Don't introduce a huge cast of characters in the opening scenes of the first chapter. Give the reader space to get to know the main characters.

The sleuth, plus those selected friends and family who will become the sidekicks for our sleuth during the investigation, all need to be on stage during Act One – but not in the opening pages unless it is essential.

Too many characters will confuse the reader and they lose track of who is who and has to keep flicking back to work out the relationships. This is annoying.

If you want to increase the pace of a fast read, my suggestion is to have the sleuth and at most two other people in a scene. This gives you the space to really bring on those extra characters and reveal their personality as they interact with your sleuth. One to one is better.

Quickly establish the setting, period, tone, style and point of view of the story.
By the end of the first scene the reader should know precisely where they are and can visualise the setting. This locks them into the world stage on which your story will be played.

Case Study Worked Example. Spite Pairs with White

Story Beat. The ordinary working and daily life of the character.

Deli owner Erin Kelly is discussing the menu for the Kingsmede Wine Festival with local winemaker and personal friend Margot Fraser, who has asked Erin to provide the catering for the Festival. Erin has worked hard to match the white wine being served with a selection of savoury and sweet canapes and Margot is delighted with the results.

Incorporate some familiar elements into the storyworld.

Erin loves the warmth of her kitchen where she creates stunning baked goods and breads every day. She knows her regular customers and has carried on her father's tradition and made the deli a meeting place.

Start with the sleuth to tell the reader that this is the person they are going to identify with and follow on their journey.

Erin is the star here – she is driving the action.

Story Beat. The internal conflict of the character [The personal conflict plot]

Erin's mother and extended family cannot understand why a talented chef and sommelier like Erin wants to stay and run her late father's Italian deli. She is still mourning the loss of her father 18 months earlier. They are nagging her to leave and move to London or Florida where the Rossi family have restaurants, a yacht catering business and hotel contracts.

Let the reader know in the first scene/first chapter who this main character is and why they should care what happens to them. Let the reader empathise and sympathise with that character and relate to them in some way.

Erin wants to build up her catering business, specialising in matching food and wine, and open her own bistro next to the deli. She would love to expand but needs to generate the finance to pay for expansion and refurbishment.

The Wine Festival is now a major event in the Hampshire food and wine calendar and the perfect chance for her to demonstrate what Kelly's Deli can deliver.

Show that she [and it is usually a she although it does not have to be] is skilled and has talents and strengths and can handle herself. She might be a "fish out of water" in this story world, but she has to be intelligent and equal or better than the murderer.

Erin is a classically trained chef and sommelier who is an expert in matching food and wine. She is also used to handling tough situations and is determined to make the deli a success.

Don't make the sleuth too perfect. Perfect and bland = boring. What flaws does she have? What are her trigger points? What are her inner conflicts? How has she made mistakes? If she had made a life changing decision, that decision must be justified morally.

She can be a hot head and totally stubborn when it comes to getting what she wants. She has put the work before her family who needs her. Later she will be challenged to make a wrong decision, but she turns away from that.

HOOK the reader in the first few paragraphs by hinting at a turning point or crisis in the sleuth's life. Why is the sleuth at the end of their tether when the story begins? This character is going to go on a journey, so she has to start in a place where she does not want to be. Start with action or dialogue to draw the readers into the story.

Erin has spent the last 12 years of her life working as a celebrity caterer and private chef. Other chefs don't understand why Erin left very successful catering business and came back to run the family deli she inherited from her late father. She needs this time to rebalance after so much loss.

Story Beat. Continuity plot with friends and members of the local community. Erin grew up in Kingsmede and has three great female friends who still live close by. Her best friend, Prisha Patel, is a lecturer at the local college and they meet up several times a week.

Sequence 2. Catalyst/Inciting Incident/Problem or New Opportunity

This is the first major spark of conflict in the story.

This is also the starting point for the A plot, the murder mystery, even if the incident is only linked to the murder.

The INCITING INCIDENT is the first significant event that completely disrupts and alters the characters life.

It could be a new opportunity but in a cozy murder mystery it is more likely to be the discovery of the first murder victim or a challenge or problem linked to the central murder investigation.

- Scene where future victim interacts with suspect – or show the body.
- Something happens which throws the sleuth's world into turmoil. It could be a murder/attack or some shocking crime.
- Why is she involved in this murder investigation? Is she a suspect or is a relative or friend a suspect? Did she discover the body?

Foreshadowing, Introduction of Stakes and Threat, Intertwined with Setup and crime to come.

This Opportunity/Problem steers the story in a new direction and hints at bigger obstacles to come as the sleuth struggles to deal with the new disruption to their life.

The most common technique for grabbing the attention of a reader is through the use of curiosity. Most successful mysteries begin by posing a puzzle to the audience, raising questions in their minds, and promising an answer.

That first question is triggered by what happens in the Inciting Incident.

Case Study Worked Example. Spite Pairs with White

Erin is serving canapes at the Wine Festival and everything is going well. She has just met her pal Amy whose father Roger is a local winemaker. His sparkling wines have taken the best wine award for the past seven years.

Suddenly Margot's husband Simon Fraser walks in with a new winemaker and Amy and her father are stunned. Simon has hired a top French wine maker and he is personal friend of the main judge.

Erin serves Simon a selection of gluten-free canapes and he gobbles them down.

When the judge awards the best wine prize to Simon Fraser, Roger accuses him of cheating and bribing the judge and storms out.

Only minutes later, Simon collapses to floor, fighting to breathe. He is severely allergic to peanuts and the ambulance crew cannot save him.

Sequence 3. Reaction to the Crime or Incident

Refusal of the call to action.

The sleuth has to try and deal with the problem of the inciting incident and is struggling to know what best to do and how to react to this disruption in her normal life.

The *Three Bumps and a Push* technique is a useful story structure tool from screenwriter David Siegel.

At first, the sleuth does not want to get anywhere near this sudden death. The sleuth debates what to do with her sidekicks/pals or family. She might resist the call at first– she is not the person to get involved.

She will refuse to get involved at the start and may need three gentle, or not so gently, nudges or '**Bumps**' to convince her to change her mind before there is one larger trigger event, the '**Push**' that makes her agree to investigate this murder.

Use the *Three Bumps and a Push* technique to quickly sketch out why the sleuth does not want to get involved and what will make her change her mind.

In a cozy they should be linked to the character relationships between the sleuth and at least one "stakes character" they care about.

By linking the crime to the backstory and internal needs of the sleuth the crime or murder becomes personal, thereby increasing the stakes.

Does the sleuth have a mentor or sidekick or friend? The mentor character encourages the sleuth and reassures them that they can cope and be strong.

The sleuth tries to resolve the situation but is blocked.

Establish the stakes. What happens if the sleuth doesn't react to this incident? Who would care?

Case Study Worked Example. Spite Pairs with White

Erin knows that none of her food contained peanuts and Margot tasted them all personally, but she is immediately under suspicion since the victim collapsed immediately after eating her food.

Bump 1. Marcel, the French wine judge accuses her of poisoning the victim.

Bump 2. James Fraser, Margot's son, accuses Erin of killing his father.

Bump 3. One of her regular clients cancelled her catering order for the coming week.

Sequence 4. First Turning Point, Core Story Launch. Break into Act Two.

Some major new event forces the sleuth to take actions that will directly impact upon their life.

This is an unexpected moment where something shifts, and it becomes imperative for the sleuth to commit to investigating this death.

At this point the sleuth has to commit to solving the crime/story question.

There is no going back now. They are fully on board. The sleuth has no choice. They have to get involved. They must be strongly motivated and have personal stakes in the investigation.

This turning point is often called the First Plot Point since the main murder mystery A story begins here.

The murderer or criminal has shattered the balanced and ordered life of the sleuth and the local community.

- The stakes have been set high. The sleuth commits to the investigation.
- The crime/murder and the cast of characters have all been introduced.
- Give the sleuth the tools she needs to talk to suspects and investigate the crime.
- How does she find out who the likely suspects are?
- Let the readers know that these people are all harbouring secrets.

- Put those likeable characters at risk. Make the stakes real for the sleuth – what does she stand to lose if she does not find the killer? Make her DRIVE the action, not just respond to it.

The Main Dramatic Question is posed.

This is the point at which we "see" what will happen in the rest of the story, and we know the story will be over when the sleuth discovers the identity of the killer.

Will the detective find out the truth about the murder of the first victim?

Foreshadowing.

The detective sets out to get to the truth and the reader knows that the sleuth will meet the killer face to face by the end of the story.

SPITE PAIRS WITH WHITE
BY SOPHIE BRENT

Case Study Worked Example. Spite Pairs with White

Push. Erin goes to visit Margot at her home after the festival. She is in shock and distraught. Her marriage was over, but she still loved Simon.

Margot Fraser asks Erin to investigate the death of her husband Simon and she promises to do whatever she can.

ACT TWO

Act Two, sequences 5 to 8.

The sleuth interviews the suspects and delves deeper into their motives/psyche. Everyone is a suspect as potential motives are unveiled. Suspects reveal alibis, tell lies and lead the sleuth in the wrong direction.

- Meetings. Casual encounters or unexpected contacts.
- Informant who wants to get paid or get even with one of the other suspects.
- Trick someone into revealing their relationship with the victim by bluffing or emotional blackmail or provocation or argument.
- Characters confide in her and offer news about other suspects.
- Sleuth has a friend who can supply technical data. Following a paper trail is another way of discovering buried details.
- Another murder or huge event linked to the backstory of the victim and suspects.
- Reveal motives of the suspects and the subplots.
- How does she get away with interviewing the suspects? Chatting with people?

There is often a small pinch point in the middle of Act Two that leads to a change of direction, a new set of witnesses and a second suspect. At the end of Act Two, that suspect is ruled out.

- Time bombs raise suspense – a ticking clock with a deadline.
- Isolate the sleuth – alone and out of range makes things scarier.
- Show the reader how the sleuth identifies suspects and solves the puzzle.

At the end of Act Two there will be a major event which causes the story to pivot in a new direction. At this point the sleuth has to recommit finding the truth. No going back from this point. **This is the Midpoint of No Return.**

This can be another murder or attack etc. as the criminal's plan gets the upper hand and the sleuth's task becomes much harder.

Act Two also introduces a B plot, such as a romance subplot.

Let's break this down into more detail.

Sequence 5. The Investigation Begins

The sleuth has to negotiate this strange new world she has agreed to be part of.

These scenes introduce the allies, friends, sidekicks, and team that she will be working with, as well as potential enemies and suspects.

How does she find out who the likely suspects are?

Motives include: fear that secrets could be revealed, hatred for someone or something, thwarted desire for something, desire for justice/fight against injustice, revenge and retribution.

The obvious suspect seems to have a great alibi, but then that alibi is ruled out. Suspects act out their external facades, but who are they under the surface?

Let the readers know that these people are all harbouring secrets.

Put those likeable characters at risk. Make the stakes real for the sleuth – what does she stand to lose if she does not find the killer? Make her DRIVE the action, not just respond to it.

Why is this crime personal for the protagonist? She has to move forward. This is a commitment and there is no going back.

She has to have flaws. Professional athletes for example are well known for being obsessive. They do not give up no matter what the psychological price.

Keep to the rules of the game between you and the reader so that they can work through the clues with the sleuth to find the murderer. The crime must be credible. Facts must be correct.

I like to think of this as collecting together all of the pieces of a jigsaw puzzle when you still don't have the picture on the box.

Tension increases and plot begins to form as the sleuth starts to understand the conflict and the motivation of the antagonist.

Use contrasts between sleuth and the sidekick who interprets the clues and also distracts the reader from the real clue by taking you in the wrong direction.

- The sleuth has now made a commitment to solving the mystery and tracking down the killer/attacker responsible for the crime.
- All of the allies and sidekicks are brought in. The sleuth assembles the investigation team, all with different quirks and characters.
- They interview key suspects and start to compile a picture of what really happened with the first crime.
- All of the possible suspects have to be identified, who appear to have had motive, means and opportunity to commit the crime.
- Then the sleuth questions them, and they seem to be making real progress.
- One of these suspects will turn out to be the actual killer.
- The suspects have alibis, tell lies or reveal clues that point to another real killer. There will be real evidence which turns out to be distraction clues, but also real revelations which indicate that the solution goes a lot deeper than they had expected.
- It soon becomes clear that a number of people wanted the victim dead, and several could have done it, but did not have the means or opportunity.

Sequence 6. Balancing Sub-Plot

- To balance out the mystery A plot, a second B plot can be introduced. This can be a romance or secondary plot, linked to the main plot in some way.
- As part of the B plot, the sleuth's background is revealed as the sub-plot is developed. Tell the reader what missing in the sleuth's life and their internal conflict and needs.
- Show how skilled the sleuth is in her ordinary world and as she talks to people. She is gaining some respect in the community and perhaps begrudging

acceptance from people who did not take her seriously or remembered her from past experiences.

Minor Pinch Point.

At the end of this step, there is often a ramp up in conflict where the real killer shows the sleuth that they are very much still in charge. She is going to have to step up and show that she can handle the challenge.

This often a character development scene where the sleuth has to shake off her former life and step more fully into the new role of being a sleuth.

Sequence 7. Motives and Secrets revealed.

- Everyone is a suspect as potential motives are unveiled.
- Make the suspects as clever and as devious as the sleuth so that they are worthy opponents.
- Characters confide in her and offer news about other suspects as they realise that the sleuth is serious.
- Sleuth often has a friend or a sidekick who has their own way of discovering buried details. Additional problems and information emerge that have to be dealt with.

Sequence 8. Midpoint of No Return.

About halfway through the book there could be another murder or serious attack or other event around end of Act Two.

Something unexpected occurs, such as the appearance of a second body, the death of a major suspect, or discovery of evidence which clears the most likely suspect. The story must take a new direction.

This is a major new development, huge revelation, and a serious new threat from the killer and his or her accomplices if they have them. This drives the next section of the book and provides new clues.

- This event could be the disappearance of one or more s[...] information emerges.
- New motives and suspects.
- In many cases, this second murder or crime was not pla[nned] but was a spontaneous event caused by the investigation [...] witness or unexpected revelation.
- Because this second crime was not planned, this can lead to careless evidence left at the crime scene or additional clues for the sleuth that can be linked to the first murder.
- Sleuth has to make a major decision. This is the point of no return and there is no going back. But it is increasingly dangerous. The stakes have increased, and more people are being hurt. Do they carry on?

Up to now our sleuth may have been reacting to the clues and revelations about the first crime in Act One and feeling that things are spinning out of their control.

Now they have to do something that it totally outside of their comfort zone before more people are hurt.

They might not know how to achieve this, but they are fired up and determined to find this killer-no matter what the personal cost it. No going back. Bridges are burnt.

ACT THREE

Sequences 9 to 12

'The Bad Boys Close In' and 'The Killer's "Evil Plan" is put in motion.

More evidence is revealed as the stakes increase.

Conclusions and reactions to the evidence, and possible suspects at this point, shift and change as more information is collated. Some suspects are eliminated.

Sequence 9. The Killer is Blocking the Investigation

After the shock of the Major Turning point at the Mid-Point end of Act Two, the characters will have to regroup and come up with a new plan in response to this new attack /new death.

This is the pivotal point in the story where it become evident that the sleuth was on the wrong track. They need to change the focus and scope of the investigation after what happened.

This new crime is critical to the case – it provides vital information. This major plot twist sends the sleuth off in a new direction.

Layers are peeled away until the real killer is at the centre.

- More interviews. Follow up on alibis and clues and gather info on the second murder. Suspects refute evidence pointing to them from the first murder.
- Moment of danger for the sleuth or moment of increased tension/hostage etc. leading to the story climax.
- The second murder or crime leads a trail of evidence to one of the suspects. New motives and suspects are revealed.
- Give some time for reaction and reflection in between the action scenes. Use the sidekick and romance subplots for this.

- Reveal hidden motives and secrets for the key suspects. This could be linked to previous clues and revelations.
- Secret relationships come to light, such as business arrangements, romantic involvement's, scores to be settled or previously unknown connections between characters.
- Develop and expose meanings of matters hinted at in Act One, to slowly clarify the significance of earlier clues.

Sequence 10. More Complications. Stakes increase.

The sleuth is blocked and goes over what they know so far with the sidekicks and other investigators so that all the options are explored.

Some major new revelation has to be explored, but they do not seem to be getting any closer to finding the killer.

Have they missed the crucial piece of information? Or misinterpreted the information they already have?

The killer uses clever misdirection to put them on the wrong track.

MORE COMPLICATIONS, HIGHER STAKES AND SUBPLOTS

The goal is harder to achieve than the sleuth thought and is tested more than she ever expected.

More things go wrong. The suspect in the second crime is innocent but framed etc.

The sleuth reveals the results of the investigation. The reader, as well as the protagonist and other characters, are given an opportunity to review what is known and assess the possibilities.

OR there is a major plot twist that sends sleuth off in a new direction.

Give her the means and/or skills early in the story to make these actions believable.

The solution of the crime appears to be impossible. Attempts to solve the crime have blocked the sleuth. Misinterpretation of clues or mistaken conclusions have led him or her in the wrong direction.

Complications/higher stakes. Bad boys plan to get away with it.

Minor Pinch Point.

At the end of this step, there is often a ramp up in conflict where the real killer and/or their helpers shows the sleuth that they are very much still in charge.

The sleuth is getting too close – they need to scare them off.

This is often a character development scene where the sleuth has to dig deeper, work more closely with her team and sidekicks, and become more assertive.

Sequence 11. Suspects narrowed down.

The sleuth starts to discover more about the real killer and their motivation.

More secrets are revealed, and the number of suspects narrowed down as the real crime becomes clearer.

The focus shifts as more evidence come to light about what happened in the second attack/murder and how it links to the first.

The killer was careless in the second attack and left behind a crucial clue which nobody has picked up on until now. The real chain of events starts to emerge.

CULMINATION TOWARD THE MAIN PLOT

The conclusion of one dramatic tension and the start of a new one.

The sleuth moves inexorably closer to his goal and discovers new info and better understanding of the nature of the opposition before him.

The killer is aware of the sleuth's actions and takes actions to prevent them from learning the truth about the conflict and obstacles the sleuth is trying to overcome. The focus shifts from subplots to the main plot.

- Sleuth makes some progress based on revelations about the murder victim(s) and their lifestyles.
- Sleuth discovers a betrayal or other new motivation for the murder.
- Sleuth uncovers the true "Evil Plan".
- All the secrets are revealed. Number of suspects narrowed down.
- Layers are peeled away until the real killer is at the centre. Reveal the chain of events which provoked the crime.

The crucial evidence is something overlooked in Act One, which appeared to have been of little consequence at the time it was first disclosed. That evidence takes on new meaning with information disclosed in Act Three.

The sleuth (and perhaps the reader, if a keen observer) becomes aware of the error which remains undisclosed to the other characters.

Sequence 12. APPARENT DEFEAT – all is lost.

There is a huge set-back for the sleuth.
- The killer's plan is working, and all seems lost. Perhaps someone betrays the sleuth, or they are threatened/people they care about are hurt.
- Their whole investigation seems to fall apart, but they cannot give up at this point, they have come too far to see the killer escape.
- Moment of danger for the sleuth or moment of increased tension etc.
- This has to be a huge turning point which forces the sleuth to change tactics and give a new response to the threat from the killer.

This is the beginning of the way back where they push against the killer.

Everything fails and blows up big-time in their face.

The greatest set back of the story for the sleuth.

It appears as if achieving the goal is impossible, but the sleuth has no choice but to try because he will have an even worse fate should he abandon his quest now.

The sleuth's internal needs/flaws are confronted defining their character arc.

- Increased threat to the sleuth.
- This leads to a huge reveal with an increased sense of hopelessness. Often comes when the opposition is hidden, and the killer's ally is suddenly revealed.
- Moment of danger for the sleuth or moment of increased tension or hostage etc leading to the story climax. Chase/escape/setbacks.

Dark Night of the Soul.
The sleuth is at their lowest point. Suicide? Smell of fear.

- The sleuth is confronted with a choice of whether to stay in the investigation or accept that they can never get to the truth, defeated, with the killer still at large.
- Large turning point which forces the sleuth to change tactics and give a new response to the threat from the killer.

Act Three ends with some shocking revelation about the killer.

The sleuth discovers a hidden truth that turns everything on its head. They have been going about this totally wrong.

Now it is time to get serious.

This is the beginning of the way back where they push against the killer.

ACT FOUR

Sequences 13 to 16

Reconstruction of what happened on that day of the murder.

Final interview and confession.

The grand finale.

Sequence 13. Heroine sleuth gets her mojo back and is back on track.

They have to completely change direction and move forward or give up.

What have they been missing? And just how much is the sleuth willing to sacrifice to get to the truth?

If possible, link this self-revelation to a personal character flaw in the sleuth so that the final resolution is linked to their personal character arc.

The sleuth evaluates the clues, evidence and information gleaned from the other characters.

- The sleuth discovers a secret about one or more of the suspects which sets them on a new path that will lead to the real killer.
- All secrets revealed. The killer's motivation has to be powerful – why they did it, who helped them, how and when.
- More complications and setbacks. They need the evidence to prove that their suspect is the killer etc.

The final puzzle piece falls into place in the form of a history lesson which forces the sleuth to completely change direction.

The history lesson answers the question *why*?

- Why is the bad guy bad?
- Why is he doing what he's doing?
- Why is he so good at it?
- Why has he started now?

The key to this scene is evidence. Most of the clues and revelations should have been picked up already during the investigation. Now they make sense.

It's just the last thing that has to fall into place for everything to make sense, and we finally learn the killer's motivation.

If there's a mastermind, he could be revealed or confronted in this scene, but not defeated. He is at the height of his power. He or she is about to execute the plan they have been dreaming about for so many years.

Only one thing can stop him. A sleuth who knows what's actually going on for a change.

She is no longer on her back foot, but she now has to drive toward the solution, usually by escaping the trap first.

What to look for:

- The story or flashback of the seminal incident.
- The oldest bit of backstory.
- Everything stopping so the sleuth can learn the history lesson.

Sequence 14. A New Action Plan

She has a sudden revelation about a clue and suspect and realizes that she been going about things in the wrong way.
She needs a new action plan and has to work quickly.
The friends, family and allies come together to create a plan. They agree to go forwards, even if there is only a small chance of success.

Sequence 15. The Grand Finale.

This is usually a one-to-one confrontation with the killer where the sleuth demonstrates their skills and wins the day.

With resolve and determination, the sleuth and the allies battle to discover the killer, who does not make it easy for them.

Just when everything seems lost, the sleuth finds the strength to unlock the secret weapon in a sudden twist and the killer is finally revealed.

Make the final confrontation with the villain slow.

Reveal every heartbeat, every pulse pounding moment of fear.

The pacing must be quick, but you should not cheat the reader out of emotional reactions, either during the scene or afterwards. Don't rush the fight scene.

Top Tip. Make the final battle with the killer real. No silly heroics.

No going down into the cellar with the lights out. This has to be a battle of equals in order for the reader to feel satisfied that the killer was caught using logic, deduction, and intelligence.

Sequence 16. Resolution.

Has to be a solid resolution which makes sense to the reader. Strong ending.

After the villain has been defeated, have a wrap up scene where the sleuth had a quiet moment with friends/sidekick/love interest or family as they review events.

Sleuth discusses clues with her family and friends and reveals how she solved the case.

Plot-B: Scene showing full character growth of the sleuth. The sleuth comes to a realisation about herself which demonstrates the character growth/character arc which occurs because she steps outside her comfort zone to investigate this death.

SHOW the sleuth back in the old world as a different person. A static sleuth who never changes will lose readers interest over time.

Use the last chapter to tie up the loose ends and perhaps frame/bookend the story to match the opening sequence. The mystery has to be completely solved – but maybe add a hint or a hook for the next story in the series.

HOW TO WRITE THE FIRST DRAFT IN TEN STEPS

My Ten-Step Procrastination-Busting Process.

Big disclaimer here. There is no ideal or perfect way to write fiction.

There is only your way, your process, your words, your approach, your style. Every writer has to work out their own writing method that is unique to them.

What I am sharing here is my personal process, which is based on my own extensive study of story craft and my practical experience creating multiple romance and crime novels.

This process can be applied to any fiction project but works particularly well for crime fiction where a detective plotline is combined with character arcs to create an engaging emotional journey for your reader.

I believe that this process is the fastest way to get to the heart of your story.

	HOW TO WRITE THE FIRST DRAFT OF A COZY MYSTERY
1	Expand the 3 Hooks and a Sleuth idea.
2	Decide on your Target Wordcount.
3	Consider what Point of View you want to write in.
4	Create a Memorable Sleuth.
5.	Who is the First Murder Victim?
6.	Who are the Possible Suspects?
7.	Character Development for the Murderer.
8.	Use scene cards to write a "discovery" first draft of Act One.
9.	Sanity check after writing the Opening Scenes.
10.	Write down Ideas for the next Key Plot Turning Points.

How to Use the Ten-Step Process

Okay. You have now come up with an amazing high-concept story idea that is cool, different, intriguing, and so interesting that you cannot wait to find out where your characters will take you.

The next step from having a basic story concept is to create the expanded premise of your book. When you have a short premise, you can use this to create the expanded outline and story points that will deliver an amazing story.

So, we have a great hook, a solid story situation and a sleuth who will investigate the murder.

At this point we are ready to get to work on the core of the story – the murder mystery puzzle.

I recommend using this step-by-step process to get to the heart of the murder mystery as fast as possible.

This really is the fun part of the writing process when you can create dozens of murder scenarios and go to town on cool and engaging ideas that are a perfect fit for both your sleuth and your story situation.

By working quickly through your ideas and options, you can triage the results and select one idea to focus on.

Once you have worked through these steps, you can then start working on a draft outline for the story using a 4-Act story structure.

This structure creates checkpoints for your story and helps you to control both the pacing and the plot, but still has enough flexibility to allow the story to pivot if your characters take the story in a more exciting direction.

HOW TO WRITE THE FIRST DRAFT OF A COZY MYSTERY	
1	Expand the 3 Hooks and a Sleuth idea.

STEP ONE. Expand the 3 Hooks and a Sleuth idea

The goal is to expand the story into a few paragraphs that you could use:

- As a back-cover blurb for the book.
- As the online book description for the book if you are self-publishing.
- As your pitch in a submission query letter to a literary agent.
- As your north star when you are writing the opening chapters and outlining the rest of the book. You are pitching the book to yourself!

I know that you are desperate to get words on paper, but I have found that it is always worth spending a few hours developing your storyline and capturing the tone, style and key character and plot elements in a few short paragraphs.

Brainstorm all of your ideas and get them onto paper. Then summarise those ideas as though you were describing what your book is about to a complete stranger.

You are making a promise to a reader about what they can expect to find in the pages of your book.

This promise has to be subgenre specific. If you are writing paranormal or historical cozy mysteries, for example, the specific genre tropes should be included. These elements will instantly signal to a reader that you know and love books in this niche and understand what they are looking for.

Note – this is not a synopsis where you outline the entire story. These paragraphs are there to sell your book, and the first person they have to convince is you!

If your short description doesn't light a fire in your belly for this story, then stop and rework it and add in new ideas until you are totally fired up to write it.

At this point the book blurb is very much a working document that you will be coming back to as you create your first draft. You never know where your characters are going to take you!

SPITE PAIRS WITH WHITE
BY SOPHIE BRENT

Case Study Worked Example. Spite Pairs with White

3 Hooks and A Sleuth Story Idea. Reminder of the Core Story Idea

Who is the sleuth? What do they do and why are they in this murder mystery?
Erin Kelly owns an Italian deli in a small English country village. She runs a catering business specialising in matching wine and food.
Hook 1. How does the sleuth get involved in the murder investigation?
Erin has made the food for a prestigious wine festival and the owner dies from a peanut allergy after eating her canapes.
How is this different and new is some way?
What if? Erin has spent the last 15 years working in top kitchens around the world before returning to her hometown. She is used to taking control and not taking no for an answer. Erin needs to build up her business and now she is being accused of causing the death at her first serious catering event. The real killer is not going to win!
Hook 2. What are the main themes of the book?
Culinary. Contemporary cozy mystery. Private Investigators.
Hook 3. What emotional experience does this book promise to deliver?

> Fun, fast paced, escapist read with good friends, food and wine in a charming English village, complete with thatched cottages.

Case Study Worked Example. Expanded Book Description

Spite Pairs with White. Gordon Ramsey meets The Thursday Murder Club.

Instead of spending the summer serving salads to A listers on a superyacht in the Indian ocean, caterer Erin Kelly is back where she started in the small Hampshire town of Kingsmede.

The annual Wine Festival is a major event in the local calendar, and no one is looking forward to it more than Erin Kelly, who is providing the catering for the award ceremony.

This is the perfect opportunity for Erin to promote the delicious food she serves at the Italian deli she inherited from her father.

Except that Erin hasn't even served her desserts, when her celebrity client keels over in front of his VIP festival guests only minutes after eating her canapes.

The last thing Erin needs is negative publicity, but when she is accused of the murder, Erin has no choice but to find the real killer before it's too late.

Secrets have been buried deep in Kingsmede, but someone is determined to rock this sleepy little town with the truth, no matter what the cost.

#But who would want to murder a part-time wine maker like Simon Fraser?

#Just how many secrets have the Fraser family been keeping quiet about all these years?

#Oh, and is making chocolate hen party treats a good idea in a village like Kingsmede?

One way or another, this is not going to be the restful summer that Erin had expected.

This is my working draft of the book description and I hope that you can see that these few paragraphs:

- Captures the voice and style of the book.
- Asks questions in the minds of the readers that will intrigue them.
- Clearly sets out the personal background of our sleuth and the type of small English town that she is coming back to.
- Establishes the subgenre. Contemporary, fun culinary mystery.

HOW TO WRITE THE FIRST DRAFT OF A COZY MYSTERY	
1	Expand the 3 Hooks and a Sleuth idea.
2	Decide on your Target Wordcount.

STEP TWO. Decide on your Target Wordcount.

Is this book going to be a short novel at 40,000 to 60,000 words or a full-length novel at 70,000 to 90,000 words?

A shorter book means that there is not a lot of room to indulge in more than two murders at most, and there will be very little narrative text. These books are fast-paced page-turners built directly around the spine of the book that is the murder investigation.

In a longer, full-length novel at 70,000 to 90,000 words you have the space to include long-running continuity subplots, multiple murders and high-stakes action scenes and more complex plotting.

The wordcount also determines where the major turning points in the Four Acts of your novel will be.

For example. Let's say that the ideal length of your first draft is around 64,000 words.

If you use the Four Act, 16 Sequence structure I have described, then each Sequence of Scenes will be on average around 4,000 words long [64,000/16].

4,000 words could be one long chapter or two shorter chapters – and this is an average over the entire book so some scenes will be longer and some shorter.

Four of these 4,000-word Sequences then build into an Act.

For example. **The turning point at the end of Act One** when the sleuth commits to investigating the crime would come at roughly 16,000 words [4 x 4,000 words]. **The Midpoint of No Return at the end of Act Two** would come at roughly 32,000 words.

The Dark Night of the Soul at the end of Act Three would come at roughly 48,000 words. **The Final Battle and Resolution at the end of Act Four** would bring the wordcount up to 64,000.

Please remember that these word counts are only there as guidelines while you are writing the first draft, but they can be very useful markers.

It is very easy to write 25,000 words before the murder investigation gets started at the end of Act One and then scrabble around for 10, 000 words for the other three Acts which don't go anywhere.

I hope that you will agree that breaking a novel down into 4,000-word sections takes away some of the overwhelm and makes the project seem more feasible.

HOW TO WRITE THE FIRST DRAFT OF A COZY MYSTERY	
1	Expand the 3 Hooks and a Sleuth idea.
2	Decide on your Target Wordcount.
3	Consider what Point of View you want to write in.

STEP THREE. Point of View

Think about your "keeper shelf" of mystery books.

What point of view do you enjoy reading most?

Point of view is the "eye" through which you tell your story. The same story can be very different when seen through another character's eyes.

This is why selecting your point of view at the start can save you a lot of time and energy later if you discover that your initial approach doesn't work for this particular writing project.

What does this look like in practice? Read back through the opening chapters of your favourite cozy mysteries with your author's hat on and analyse how that author hooked you into the story through their use of point of view.

First Person Point of View

Here are some examples of how cozy mystery authors have used first-person point of view in the opening paragraphs of their work.

Worked Example. The Vampire Knitting Club by Nancy Warren

My grandmother, Agnes Bartlett, owned the best knitting shop in Oxford and I was on my way to visit her after spending a very hot month at a dig site in Egypt with my archeologist parents.

I was looking forward to telling Gran about my latest life crisis. I might be twenty-seven years old and supposedly all grown up, but Gran was always ready to wrap her warm arms around me and tell me everything was going to be all right. I needed comforting after discovering my boyfriend of two years, Todd, had stuck his salami in someone else's sandwich. I referred to him now as my ex-boyfriend 'The Toad.'

[My thanks to Nancy Warren for granting permission to use this extract.]

Worked Example. Witch is When It All Began by Adele Abbott

"What's that thing?" The young man looked horrified.

"That's Winky." How dare he call my darling cat a thing? Sure, Winky had only one eye, and looked as though he'd just walked off the set of a slasher movie, but deep down, underneath all that fur and latent aggression, he was sweet and adorable. At least, that's what the woman at the cat re-homing centre had told me. Gullible? Who? Me?

Winky jumped onto my desk, and immediately the young man pushed his chair back. He probably thought he'd be safe at that distance, but he hadn't seen how far Winky could jump.

"Get down!" I tried to push Winky off the desk, but he managed to avoid my arm. His meowing grew louder as he walked around in circles, directing his attention first at me and then at the young man. "Sorry about this." I forced a smile and pressed the intercom.
"

[My thanks to Implode Publishing Ltd for granting permission to use this extract.]

Advantages of using the First-Person Point of View

Many cozy mystery authors use first-person point of view to instantly engage the reader with the mindset of the main character in the story, who is usually the sleuth.

The goal of the opening scenes of any novel is to lock the sympathy and empathy of the reader with the main character and their life goals, dreams, and ordinary world.

By going straight into their head and their emotions and thoughts, you are helping readers to instantly relate to this person and the life they are leading when the story begins.

The pace and rhythm of the narrative tends to be faster using first-person point of view since all of the action is going on in real time. Everything that happens is expressed deftly and directly through the eyes and thoughts of the sleuth.

What they do, how they react to the Inciting Incident and the decisions and dilemmas they face are completely biased since they will be filtered through the emotional reactions and thought processes of this character.

The tone of first-person cozies does tend to be more conversational and approachable than third person mysteries.

Some authors like to write character notes and ideas in first person as part of the character development process, but then go on to write the novel in third person.

Disadvantages of using the First-Person Point of View.

The truth is, there are many readers who love cozy mysteries, but cannot stand to read novels told in first person. It just does not work with them and they will always use the "Look Inside" option to read the sample pages before buying. This is entirely personal preference, but you should be aware of it.

You have to be comfortable with using **me** and **I** in every sentence and working out the entire story from the actions, reactions, thoughts and decisions taken by the point of view character.

Not all sleuths are attractive characters, and you have to like being inside their heads for 50,000 words and above. This is especially true if you are planning to write a series of books with the same sleuth, set in the same story world.

If your sleuth is the kind of person who will go alone down dark alleys at night armed only with high heels and a kitten, then they could annoy the reader instead of engaging with them and their journey.

The individual idiosyncrasies and backstory of this character will have to be revealed through dialogue and in their interactions with other characters, especially the sidekicks, family and friends who will form part of the murder investigation team.

So. If you can combine the immediacy of being straight into the thoughts of the sleuth, with a compelling murder mystery, then first person could be a great choice.

Third-Person Point of View

Types of Third Person Point of View.

Close Third Person. Also known as Limited Third Person.

Here we are describing the story through the eyes of one person, or a small number of characters, one at a time. What does this look like in practice?

Worked Example. Dead Pairs with Red **by** Sophie Brent

> *Erin Kelly had an aversion to sky-blue Porsches, even before Olga Petrova side-swiped her battered old Volkswagen Golf, smashing the wing mirror, and causing the two cases of Californian Merlot in the back to rattle like a glass recycler.*
>
> *Erin should have known that things were going too well today. Half an hour earlier, she was actually on track to making it back from her delivery run in time for her own birthday party.*

Omniscient Third Person

This is when the author acts as an all-seeing and all-knowing narrator and is able to describe the thoughts and actions and decisions taken by every character in the story and does so in narrative style. It also allows the author to introduce aspects of the story that could not be described by the characters themselves.

This can be a very useful technique and was a standard device in historical novels, although present tense omniscient third person can also be used.

What does this look like in practice?

Example text of Present Tense Omniscient Third Person. (A made-up example)

She opens the front door using the key kept under the planter on the porch and steps inside the cold bungalow. There is no answer when she calls her uncle's name and as she pushes open the kitchen door, Kathy knows instantly that something is wrong. She enters the room and turns off the radio that is set to a loud rock music station. Her uncle Pat hates rock music.

Worked Example of Omniscient Third Person .

The opening from Crime and Punishment by Fyodor Dostoevsky

> *He had successfully avoided meeting his landlady on the staircase. His garret was under the roof of a high, five-storied house and was more like a cupboard than a room. The landlady who provided him with garret, dinners, and attendance, lived on the floor below, and every time he went out, he was obliged to pass her kitchen, the door of which invariably stood open. And each time he passed, the young man had a sick, frightened feeling, which made him scowl and feel ashamed. He was hopelessly in debt to his landlady and was afraid of meeting her.*

Advantages of Third Person Point of View

Multiple Points of View

If you have two main characters in your book, such as the sleuth and, for example, the private investigator or police officer who is helping her, then it can be very useful to have scenes where each of these two characters views the murder investigation from their unique perspective.

Some crime writers allow the murderer to have their own point of view so that the reader is one step ahead of the sleuth during the investigation.

Personally, I would not have more than two points of view in a cozy mystery, unless it is a full-length novel, and each voice is very distinctive. In this case, I would label each chapter with the name of the character who is speaking so the reader is not confused by the break in style and voice.

> **Key Tip. If you are using third person point of view, stay with one point of view per scene.**

There is nothing more distracting and confusing that reading a scene and suddenly finding that you have "head hopped" into the viewpoint of another character. You can switch to the viewpoint of the other person inside the same chapter by adding a scene break, but only if it is absolutely essential and does not confuse the reader.

Disadvantages of Third Person Point of View

The third person omniscient present tense narration can keep at reader at arm's length from the main characters. This is particularly important in the main turning point scenes when the energy and dramatic and emotional tension of the scene can be lost.

The detailed emotional connection to the characters and their internal thoughts is reserved for dialogue and actions/reactions which reveal their internal processes.

It also means that there tends to be long passages of background narration about the characters and lots of head hopping which could be difficult to track at times.

Combining Different Points of View in the same Book.

Worked Example. In **The Thursday Murder Club**, **Richard Osman** tells the story through the personal journal and multiple viewpoints of the main characters.

He uses the viewpoints of our sleuth Joyce in the first person when she is writing in her journal, local police constable Donna in third person, and Ian Ventham in the third person present tense omniscient.

This is a very useful technique since it makes it clear to the reader who is speaking in that particular chapter, since they each have a separate voice. Each chapter is also given the name of the character.

Research the most popular Point of View for Cozy Mysteries in your Niche.

Point of View used in the Top 50 Bestselling Mysteries on Amazon.com

Amazon Category and Subcategory	First Person	Third Person
Mystery-Cozy Animals	63%	37%
Mystery-Cozy Crafts and Hobbies	54%	46%
Mystery-Cozy Culinary	45%	55%
Suspense-Ghosts	32%	68%
Suspense-Paranormal	63%	37%

Please note – this is a snapshot of the bestseller charts at one moment in time and the chart is updated every hour or so, so always check the point of view in the books in your niche that you read and want to write.

There is one observation from this sample: traditional publishers still seem to prefer third person narratives. Many of the first-person point of view books are from independently published authors.

I prefer to use close third person which gives me the opportunity to dive deeper inside the head of the sleuth and one or two other main characters.

The golden rule is this – work with the point of view that you feel comfortable with and find easiest to write. It must fit your personal style and writing voice, or the entire book will feel forced and unauthentic.

Plus. Rewriting an entire novel from a different point of view is a lot of work.

	HOW TO WRITE THE FIRST DRAFT OF A COZY MYSTERY
1	Expand the 3 Hooks and a Sleuth idea.
2	Decide on your Target Wordcount.
3	Consider what Point of View you want to write in.
4	Create a Memorable Sleuth

You have already worked on options for your sleuth in the exercises for the Four Hook Story Generator, so you should have at least one possible idea for who your sleuth is and why they are here in this particular story world.

This is broad strokes characterisation at this stage and the goal is know just enough to bring the character onto the story stage, acting and reacting and talking about what matters to them.

STEP FOUR. Creating a Memorable Sleuth

Focus on one main character who will open the story - your sleuth.

You have already worked on options for your sleuth in the exercises for the Four Hook Story Generator, so you should have at least one possible idea for who your sleuth is, and why they are here in this particular story world.

This is broad strokes characterisation at this stage and the goal is to know just enough about the sleuth to bring the character onto the story stage, acting and reacting and talking about what matters to them.

There is one fundamental aspect of the cozy murder mystery genre which explains why readers come back to writers and series they love – it is all about the characters.

I like to think of it this way.

As a reader, when I buy a cozy mystery, I want to feel that I am a tourist taking a vacation in an interesting new town/city/resort for a few days. I have booked a family-run bed and breakfast hotel and the owners know everyone in the town. I am excited about who I am going to meet during my short stay and want to find out more about this town and its customs and heritage.

I want to be transported into an interesting story world where I meet warm, charming, and quirky characters I want to spend time with and get to know better. I want to listen to their stories and unique voices and dive deep into their lives.

How do I do that?

By following the journey these characters take when there is a murder in their town, and they are forced to deal with the aftermath of the crime.

One or two main characters will set out to discover who the killer is and bring them to justice before order can be restored to this small community.

In the process of investigating the murder they reveal their true nature and backstories, making me connect with them at a much deeper level.

When I finally repack my virtual suitcase and head home, I know that I will be coming back and spending more vacations in the company of this group of interesting people who have become more like old friends.

That is why I would always recommend that you plan from the start to write a series of books with the same main characters and setting. Readers come back to this story world to reconnect with these same characters and discover what has changed in their lives.

None of that matters if the reader does not care about the characters and what happens to them.

No matter what the genre, our role as an author is to bring our characters into the world of that story and then reveal the thoughts and actions of those characters when they have to deal with challenges and are forced to make difficult decisions.

In the process, the reader should feel sympathy and empathy for our main characters and want to follow their journeys. They have to care whether they will achieve their goals. And that begins with the main characters of our cozy mystery.

Select one main amateur sleuth with a unique twist.

Classically the sleuth is an ordinary person who is driven to take action to find the truth. The sleuth should fit the context of the time period and setting.

Create a network of the supporting cast of recurring friends and family in the community who will support your sleuth.

Each will have their own storyline subplot in this and other books in the series. These are the characters readers will want to meet again in the next books.

START WITH YOUR SLEUTH

This is your main character, and you should know enough about them to get them onto the page as living, breathing people.

Main Cast List
- The Amateur Sleuth
- The Sidekick(s), Friends and Family
- The Killer
- The Victim(s)
- The Suspects

Get the groundwork done before you start work on the opening scenes.

Grab some cards and capture your ideas on paper. Dialogue, plot twists, fun character traits – anything at all that you come up with for this story.

If you have used the Three Hooks and a Sleuth Story Generator you already have a spark of an idea about who your sleuth is going to be.

Why is the sleuth investigating this [first] murder? Why her? Why now? What special qualities does she have that make her an ideal sleuth?

The Amateur Sleuth

So, what characteristics are we looking for in the amateur sleuth who is going to be the main character in this book and multi-book series?

This is a story world where murders are committed and described without graphic gory details or exploding car chases.

In most modern cozies the sleuth is often:

- female
- probably at least 30 years of age but often much older to match the target demographic of your ideal reader.
- working in a skilled profession demanding years of training or has a technically demanding interest or hobby.
- she probably runs her own business or is training to run a business.
- she is single, widowed or divorced but may have older children who have left home.
- she has family, friends and co-workers who like her.
- she has her own challenges, needs and desires which have not been met so far in her life so she is open to new experiences.
- she is brave and funny.

Let's focus on a few key attributes.

Intelligence

There is a reason why modern cozy mysteries set their murders in isolated locations and small towns, far away from major cities who have dedicated homicide detectives, sophisticated forensic equipment, and elaborate databases of criminal profiling.

The sleuth must rely on their deep personal knowledge of human nature and the relationships between their friends, family, and neighbours in their local community to solve the murder.

Characters with realistic human motivations and challenges drive the murder investigation in this genre.

Your sleuth should therefore be intelligent and expert at seeing the patterns in the clues and revelations that emerge during the questions and answers.

Perhaps she is an expert "people-watcher" and has an innate ability to notice clues or recognise behaviours that the police overlook.

Flaws.

Don't make our sleuth too perfect and squeaky clean. Perfect = Boring.

What flaws does she have? What are her inner conflicts? What kind of terrible decisions has she taken in the past? What are her worst mistakes?

Resilience

Your female sleuth has to have deep inner strength – without necessarily being pushy.

Imagine that your sleuth is an ordinary person thrust into extraordinary circumstances. She could be a visitor to this town, someone returning after a long absence or a citizen thrust into a murder or crime scene.

How does she react? Panic and wave her arms about and start screaming for help? Maybe. But that would be the obvious thing to do.

Don't be predictable. Readers want to read about a sleuth who is different, so show how that react in that situation in unexpected ways.

Any adult will come onto the world of your story with a background of personal experiences of family loss and experience with the medical and legal systems where they live.

Readers love to see women who can cope with drama and conflict and come out fighting when they need to. They own their strength.

This woman is not waiting for a man to save her – she is quite capable of saving herself!

If a man wants to work with her, she might be willing to give him a chance, but she is quite prepared to work this investigation on her own.

Which leads us to:

A Romance Subplot

An alpha female thrust into a world of alpha males is going to cause some sparks to fly, which helps to add that magical energy and humour to your murder-mystery.

Two competing intellects with different approaches can lead to witty banter and interesting situations.

Perhaps your amateur sleuth is forced to work with a police officer, private detective, bodyguard, or other professional person who does not appreciate the interference from amateurs in the community.

Think of all of the TV crime shows where the male and female leads in the series have an ongoing competing relationship and a "will they/won't they" dynamic going on. From **Moonlighting to Castle, Gourmet Detective to Miss Fisher Murder Mysteries**, the combination of two mismatched but very individual characters create a powerful series energy that brings life to your story and possibly some light against the darkness of your murder or crime.

It could be a sensual vibe in a TV series, but in this genre the relationship must stay very clean with very little inuendo or crudity. Bedroom doors definitely stay closed.

Many cozy readers enjoy an ongoing romantic subplot, but others don't and actively avoid it.

If it works for your story and builds character and plot, that's great. But a romance subplot is not essential for an effective story. Many amateur sleuths are married or are in a long-term relationship or not interested in another relationship.

EXPAND ON YOUR IDEAS FOR THE SLEUTH

Why is the sleuth at a crisis or crossroads in her life when the story begins?

What internal and external conflicts are challenging her? Start with action and dialogue to draw the reader into her life.

Motivation. Why is your sleuth committed to investigate this murder?

How can you make this murder personal?

- What if someone is trying to hurt the people you love in your family, friends, or community?
- What would you do to protect them?
- Would you want to find out more about the person who is threatening them, even if this puts you in danger?

These personal connections mean that the stakes are high from the start.

Now increase those stakes – make this the worst thing that could happen to our sleuth and those she cares about.

FREE WRITING EXERCISES

Have fun and come up with several ideas on how you can introduce the sleuth character and their story world into this story.

Jot down ideas as bullet points that can be expanded later.

The reader should be able to get inside the head of each character and visualize their world in technicolour detail, step into their shoes and follow their journey to a satisfying conclusion.

How to get inside their heads?

You could use first person point of view [POV] to reveal the character's thoughts or close third person.

Their dialogue and banter with other characters. Allow the other person to reveal something about the sleuth's character.

This is a small town where people know one another, but at this point, how much of the victim's background should you reveal? It should be just enough for the reader to ask questions which will be answered later in the text.

Case Study Example. Spite Pairs with White

WHO is the Sleuth? Erin Kelly [Erin]

What does she do for a living? [Link to series hook.]

Erin runs an Italian Deli she inherited from her late father, specialising in matching food and wine. She pours her passion into her food at Kelly's deli and her close community of pals and customers/neighbours.

How old is she?

28. Erin spent her gap year with her mother and uncles in America then went to university in London including time in Italy as an intern, then worked as a private chef on luxury yachts before returning to the deli.

What are her special talents? She has to be intelligent and a match for the villain.

Intelligent. Erin is an assertive and independent and strong character. Will not be told what to do. Inherited her mother's stubborn will and her dad's kind heart. She was a private chef for Hollywood stars and business leaders before she came back to Kingsmede.

What does she want in life –her internal conflicts from her backstory.

Has just started a food blog with her own photos of her dishes and runs the deli website she created for her dad.
Does she want to do this for the rest of her life?
Is this what her parents wanted for her?
Her mother is living in Florida and trying to persuade her to sell the deli and work for her in yacht catering and the family business.

The reader should feel sympathy and empathy with the main character.

When her father had his first serious stroke, she came to stay for a few weeks and never went back to London. Her boyfriend was very supportive and used to come and stay every weekend at first, until things become difficult and she was working full-time in the deli.

He left her to start a relationship with her friend, so Erin lost her boyfriend and her friend just when she needed them. Her friends in Kingsmede have become her extended family rather than the grandparents and mother.

What are her long term and her immediate goals? What is blocking her?

To be independent of her mother's family who are trying to run her life for her and tell her what to do on a weekly basis.
Her dream is to run her own bistro as well as the deli.

Cooking and catering are all that she has known. She has so many offers and options. What does she want to do?

How is she able to talk to suspects? Kelly's Deli is a local hang out and gossip central for customers. She rents it out at night to community groups. Big tables and comfy chairs.

Does she have a pet? Erin is allergic to pet hair but loves cats. She has a pot cactus called Spike.

Give your sleuth ONE internal conflict or emotional barrier which will be the start of their character arc in this book and in a series of linked books.

This is how screenwriting coach **Michael Hauge** defines Internal Conflict:

"Internal Conflict is whatever quality within the character that prevents him from achieving real self-worth."

Give the sleuth ONE major fear or limiting belief that you can use as her internal conflict in this story.

Look into her past and chose one event which shaped the way she thinks about life- her "ghost". This is her wound, the unhealing source of continuing pain.

- How does she stop that pain from happening again? What is the one rule she lives by? How has that event informed their current controlling and limiting belief systems which sets the rules about how they live their life?
- How can this limiting belief become a barrier to her detective work?

The early life experiences of that character have led to that character's inherent system of beliefs about how the world works and their place in that world.

These controlling and sometimes limiting beliefs set the rules the character uses to make decisions in their life, especially when it comes to protecting themselves from emotional pain or loss.

When the story opens the character will come on stage with those rules and limiting belief systems all in place.

In the opening chapters the reader will only know how the character reacts to the challenges they are hit with, but it is crucial that you know the deep-seated root cause of these beliefs which are the foundation for the character's internal conflicts.

In a mystery novel we are mainly concerned with the emotional internal conflicts, but there could be several layers to these beliefs which will be revealed at the crisis key decision points in the story.

Give your sleuth ONE reason why they are at a crossroads or facing some real challenge in their ordinary life when the story opens.

This is usually the ONE thing that our sleuth wants at that moment but feels frustrated that she cannot achieve. Link this desire to the story idea to make the character come alive in that story situation. We are going to attack this character with all kinds of trouble and blocks so that they reveal who they are under pressure.

The sleuth must have a powerful and all-consuming short-term goal when the story opens which is easy to understand and for the reader to relate to.

Stakes.

The stakes for reaching that goal must be set high to make the reader care.

What would happen if the character failed to achieve their goal? Why should we care? This is a crucial element in creating believable character motivation.

How? By making the character sympathetic and empathetic.

The reader feels sympathy for their situation and empathises with their need to achieve their goal – because it could happen to us. This creates that gut emotional appeal which grabs you as a reader and makes the story feel personal.

We need the reader to identify with the character and care about the outcome of the story. So, it pays to make the character suffer and set them against overwhelming blocks to achieving their goal.

SPITE PAIRS WITH WHITE
BY SOPHIE BRENT

Case Study Worked Example from Spite Pairs with White.

Erin has been given the opportunity to start her own bistro as well as the deli, but she needs the income from a catering business to get started. Erin is determined to make this catered event at a wine tasting festival a great success and attract new business. This was her late father's dream, and he did not live long enough to make it a reality. If she cannot raise the income she will have to move away and get a full-time job in a city restaurant to raise the funds.

Give your sleuth ONE friend, family member, pet or other secondary character who is going to be their main ally for this book.

Sidekicks are super important in cozy mystery fiction. Not only do they act as someone for the detective to talk to, but they can have their own subplot which forms part of the continuity plot between other books in the same series.

Think multi-book series from the start.

Create a network of the supporting cast of recurring friends and family in the community.

Each will have their own storyline subplot in this and other books in the series. These are the characters readers will want to meet again in the next books.

Team Sleuth

- The Sleuth.
- The "Stakes Character" or characters, alive or dead, who the sleuth is emotionally connected to and who motivates the sleuth to investigate the murder. This is usually a family member, close friend, or work colleague.

They could, for example, be accused of being the killer, linked to the killer or be suffering because of this sudden death. If they are the victim, then the sleuth will investigate to bring the killer to justice.

- The Sidekicks/Helpers who are going to support the sleuth.
- The Sleuth's family members and friends.
- The local police or other officials and private investigators.
- Pets, ghosts, or other paranormal characters linked to the theme that you have chosen for your book.

SPITE PAIRS WITH WHITE
BY SOPHIE BRENT

Case Study Worked Example Spite Pairs with White

Erin's three close friends from school still live in the area. Her quirky best friend Prisha is her confident and sounding board and she knows that she can rely on Prisha to stand by her and help her out when needed.

These three steps need to be completed before the murder victim is discovered.

Why? So that the reactions of the sleuth to the murder feel real to the reader.

We understand why the sleuth feels this way, because we know who she is and what her life is like, before the bombshell of a murder blows her off her feet.

We want to see the world around her through her eyes and step into her shoes.

At this point the goal is to create a memorable character who a reader can relate to. Ideally the reader should have both empathy and sympathy for your sleuth from the start and want to find out what she does with her life.

That's why we are bringing her onto the stage of the story world as a real, living person with friends and family and personal problems to resolve, before she has to deal with a crisis.

	HOW TO WRITE THE FIRST DRAFT OF A COZY MYSTERY
1	Expand the 3 Hooks and a Sleuth idea.
2	Decide on your Target Wordcount.
3	Consider what Point of View you want to write in.
4	Create a Memorable Sleuth
5.	Who is the First Murder Victim?

STEP FIVE. The First Murder Victim

Build on your Story Idea and create a profile of the first victim and their mode of death.

- Who is the murder victim?
- Does the sleuth know the victim? This gives her a reason to get involved and care about why this murder happened.
- Was the victim likeable? How can you demonstrate this before the murder takes place so that the reader cares about this person before they are killed?
- The means of death.
- Was the sleuth present when the murder took place?
- What did the killer leave at the murder scene or remove from the scene that provides a vital clue for our sleuth?
- Why should anyone want to kill this person?
- What aspects of their past history and current behaviour will be revealed by the sleuth, which leads them directly to multiple suspects?

SPITE PAIRS WITH WHITE
BY SOPHIE BRENT

Case Study Worked Example from Spite Pairs with White

Simon Fraser is the husband of Margot Fraser, who has hired Erin to cater for the Kingsmede Wine Festival. He is a city hedge fund manager who is well known for his sharp practices. Simon and Margot have invested heavily in the wine estate Margot inherited from her parents and Simon is determined that his wine should take first prize at the Festival to impress his guests.

Simon is allergic to peanuts and collapses and dies after eating Erin's canapes – he had been deliberately poisoned.

It is no secret that Simon had to leave the city in disgrace after his earlier business failed, leaving heavy debts. Now he has sold his current firm without telling his family. He is leaving his wife and old life behind.

Expand on the Backstory of the Victim and the Motivation of the Killer

Note down at least five ideas about the backstory of the murder victim and how they came to this point in their lives. Expand more as you write the story.

Focusing on the backstory of the murder victim, including their lifestyle, friends and family will deliver a logical and rational explanation which makes sense.

If you understand why someone would want to kill the victim, then you can create multiple suspects.

Then use that background to come up at least three ideas for why someone will want to murder the victim and how they did it.

This is the start of the journey to discovering who your killer is and why the sleuth is going to have to work hard to match the killer's intelligence and determination.

You are going to need three to five possible suspects for this murder, so the more creative the ideas you can come up with at this stage the better.

For example. Let's say that there are three suspects: each one has solid motivation for wanting to kill the victim, who has been found dead at home, all linked to the character of the victim.

Example Suspect #1. A Betrayed Wife.

What is the surface motivation for killing this person? The victim had just told her that he was leaving her for another woman.

What is the deeper motivation? She believed that her husband loved her and now feels betrayed by the one person she believed that she could trust in her life.

What is the even deeper motivation? She had given up everything for this man and left her home and family behind to be with him and start a new life together. He was lying, so that he could use her money and connections so that he could advance his own career. He is now a multimillionaire. He mocks and insults her as being stupid and gullible.

What is the motivation linked to a need? Need to be loved and treasured.

Was this murder planned in advance or a sudden act of violence? Sudden act. She pushed him down the stairs as he tried to leave with his suitcase, and he broke his neck on the way down. Then she instantly called the police and ran out of the house screaming for help.

What is the killer's alibi at the time of the murder? She had come home early from a conference and found her husband packing. She is still wearing her pristine business suit when the police arrive, with her suitcases in the hall. No blood on her or her clothing. No sign of violence. Neighbours saw her arrive just before she called for help.

Example Suspect #2. Avarice

What is the surface motivation for killing this person? The victim was an old friend who had promised the killer that he would invest in his new business idea, then refused to pay when he came to him, desperate for help.

What is the deeper motivation? The killer has huge gambling debts and had borrowed money from violent men who are threatening his family. His wife has already left him for selling their possessions and they have lost their home.

The victim is an old university friend who he had helped in the past, but the victim refuses to give him any more money. He had already paid for rehab and bailed the killer out more than once before.

What is the even deeper motivation? The victim sees the killer as a weak addict who is not worthy of respect and love. He mocked the killer for not being able to hold down a job and pay his way in the world. He is a spoilt rich kid who had great education and threw it away. And the killer is clever enough to recognise that it is the truth.

How is the killer's motivation linked to a need? Self-worth and self-esteem. He is fighting for his life and his family's safety.

Was this murder planned in advance or a sudden act of violence?

Unplanned. He went to the house that afternoon to ask for help and they got into a fight. Grabbed a kitchen knife and stabbed the victim.

What is the killer's alibi at the time of the murder?

Made sure that he was seen leaving the victim's house after their meeting, waving goodbye in apparent good spirits. Did not want to stay late since he had to go to work the next day. Apparently turning his life around. Was in work early next morning.

Example Suspect #3. Planned Revenge

What is the surface motivation for killing this person? The killer wanted to stop the victim from leaving before they could be brought to justice.

What is the deeper motivation? The suspect believes that the victim was responsible for the death of a family member in a sailing accident, but he had got away with it.

What is the even deeper motivation? The victim has taunted the killer over the years and refused to admit responsibility.

What is the motivation linked to a need? Revenge and retribution for past wrongs.

Was this murder planned in advance or a sudden act of violence? Planned. They knew that the victim would be alone in his home that afternoon. Made to look like suicide because of a guilty conscience. Faked a suicide and confession note for the police and his family. Killer had worked for the victim and knows what his signature looks like.

What is the killer's alibi at the time of the murder?

Nothing to link the killer to the victim. Left no trace evidence. Used a different name, car, and disguise as a telephone engineer. Made sure that people at work in a different city had seen him that morning and evening. The timing had to be perfect to make the killing work.

I hope that you can see from these short examples that by building up a character profile for the victim, you can create endless permutations when it comes to your suspects, who all have very good reasons for wanting the victim dead.

In most mysteries, the greater the number of suspects, the more complex the puzzle, which rewards readers.

Now all you have to do is create the sequence of clues, revelations and tiny mistakes that will lead the sleuth to the possible suspects.

HOW TO WRITE THE FIRST DRAFT OF A COZY MYSTERY	
1	Expand the 3 Hooks and a Sleuth idea.
2	Decide on your Target Wordcount.

3	Consider what Point of View you want to write in.
4	Create a Memorable Sleuth
5.	Who is the First Murder Victim?
6.	Who are the Possible Suspects?

STEP SIX. The Suspects

One of the delights for any reader of cozy fiction has to be working out the identity of the real killer, from the range of possible suspects identified by our sleuth.

It is a delicious puzzle where the reward is justice for the victim and a rebalancing of the world order, in times when the real world seems to be in chaos.

My job as a writer is therefore to present the readers with a range of suspects who have convincing and credible reasons why they want the victim dead/injured. So, lots of brainstorming is required.

- **Who has most to gain from the victim's death?**
- **Give everyone a secret and a motive – from paying for a nursing home for a beloved relative to revenge to greed.**
  Passion and money are classic motives, but what about the deep secrets they are hiding?
- **Keep the motives different for each suspect but based on the relationships between people – envy, greed, revenge, resentment, fear of exposure etc.**

Develop the list of suspects and their motives, means and opportunities.

Select one suspect who is going to be the main antagonist and an equal match for the sleuth. Build up their backstory.

Recreate how the first murder was committed and then create the clues that will lead the sleuth to the killer.

Who are the suspects and how does the sleuth find the clues and revelations to their motive for killing the victim?

Here are five ideas to help you brainstorm possible suspects:

Suspect 1 – THE OBVIOUS KILLER.

Suspect 2 – THE FAMILY MEMBERS linked to the victim.

Suspect 3 – THE POSSIBLE KILLER IN THE COMMUNITY

Suspect 4 – THE OUTSIDER

Suspect 5 – THE HIDDEN SUSPECT

Of course, this list of possible suspects is only a suggestion and every mystery is unique, but I have found it useful to use these ideas for suspects as a guideline to quickly develop a story outline which is both well motivated and will create an interesting puzzle for the sleuth and the reader to solve.

Using multiple suspects in this way helps to build layers of conflict, moments of sudden exposition and character-driven emotional intensity, plus red herrings, and distractions as their connection to the victim is revealed.

Sometimes the connection will be unexpected and startling and reveal a completely new aspect of the victim's life that the sleuth knew nothing about.

Each suspect leads to, or directly provides, an additional clue or "breadcrumb" for the sleuth to follow as they follow a broken path towards the real killer.

Case Study Worked Example from Spite Pairs with White

In a short cozy mystery like Spite Pairs with White, I think four or five suspects is enough for the reader to work through, but they do have to be compelling and individual. This can work especially well when we are in a small English village in Hampshire, where people know one another – or do they?

Suspect 1 – The OBVIOUS KILLER

Suspect	Roger Fitzpatrick
Motive	Simon Fraser was threatening to take away his daughter's future and everything he had given his life to achieve.
Why now?	Simon wanted to buy Roger's vineyard for the expansion of red grapes to make his award-winning rose wine. Roger knew that Simon had bribed the festival judges so he could take Roger's supermarket contract.
Means	Roger had access to the kitchen when the food was getting ready to go out – he could have added the peanut butter to the canapes.
Secrets	Roger was once friends with Margot and Simon and had invested in one of Simon's failed business funds, leaving him with nothing but promises.
Opportunity	He knew this house and where the food was – he delivered the wine earlier that day and had plenty of time when Amy was chatting with Erin.
Alibi	He stomps out the second after Simon is give the award - shouting and angry. Amy goes after him.
Clue?	Roger shouts at Simon and accuses him of cheating.

Suspect 2 – THE POSSIBLE KILLER linked to the victim.

Suspect	Simon's wife Margot Fraser
Motive	**Her love for Simon and her home.** Simon planned to leave her and move to New York. She loves him, but he is bored here and has done what he set out to do, and he is bored with her.
Why now?	Margot discovered that Simon had sold the family business without telling her, just before the awards. That was why he was late. He wanted to get it out of the way before he got the award. Leave on a high.
Means	She feeds the wild birds finely chopped peanuts.
Secrets	Margot knew all about his past girlfriends because he told her. Not the first and certainly not the last other woman in his life. But this time he wants to leave Margot for a young American lawyer with taste in fine city life. Exactly the opposite of homely Margot and her country dogs.
Opportunity	Margot runs the kitchens. Easy to add the peanuts.
Alibi	She was walking in the woods with her dogs.
Clue?	Reveal that Simon was leaving her.

Suspect 3 – THE POSSIBLE KILLER who lives in the community.

Suspect	**James Fraser– – Simon's only son** works for the company.
Motive	**Money.** Simon sacked him and told him to get his life sorted out without the family handouts. Simon knew all about James's gambling and drug problems.
Why now?	James has returned from summer holiday to find that his father has sold the business without telling him. He is bitter and confused. They had a massive row that morning because Simon

	did not want the word getting out until he was ready to announce it to his investors.
Means	Well known that Simon was allergic to peanuts.
Secrets	James knows all of his father's dirty business secrets and suspects that he is about to leave for good but has kept quiet out of loyalty to his family.
Opportunity	James lives at the house and knows the kitchens.
Alibi	James was at the back of the room when Simon went to the front, and he had only just arrived at the festival, but he had full access to the kitchen fridges where the canapes were stored, and he was holding Simon's bag with his adrenaline injection.
Clue?	Reveal that James was sacked that day. No more bail outs from Simon.

Suspect 4 – THE OUTSIDER

Suspect	**Marcel DuBois.** The judge at the Kingsmede Wine Festival.
Motive	**Self-Protection.** Simon was threatening to destroy his reputation as a wine judge and bribed him.
Why now?	Simon had blackmailed him to turn the judges' decision his way and was getting greedy. Marcel has lost a lot of his own vineyard to a terrible fire and needs the income and to maintain his reputation.
Means	Marcel was one of Simon's clients – knows all about the peanut allergy.
Secrets	Simon had him in his pocket – he owes Simon a big favour which would ruin his career if it got out. Simon found out that Marcel had

HOW TO WRITE A COZY MYSTERY 133

	taken bribes in the past and has paid him to cheat and give his wine the award.
Opportunity	Marcel was staying at the Fraser house and had full access to the festival rooms and kitchen.
Alibi	Marcel was in the judging room when Simon ate the contaminated food.
Clue?	Simon had bribed Marcel on the day before the contest.

Suspect 5 – THE HIDDEN SUSPECT

Suspect	**Rachel Ellis.** Office manager for the Wine Growers Association
Motive	Retribution and passion. She has been Simon's mistress for the last 8 years, but Simon went back to his wife when his business collapsed. Rachel gave up her job in London and followed Simon to this small town so they could still see one another.
Why now?	Simon means to divorce his wife and marry his super rich American girlfriend. He is leaving both his wife and Rachel.
Means	Rachel was responsible for organising the Wine Festival. She slips in to help clear the tables, including Simon's plate.
Secrets	Her real name is Araminta Hargrove [Minta]. She has changed her appearance and dress. Gone back to being a brunette. Unrecognisable to anyone who had known the old Minta.
Opportunity	Nobody questions a waitress clearing tables. They are invisible, especially when the awards are just to be announced. Plus, she was on the organising committee. Familiar face.
Alibi	She had already left the room with a tray of glasses and plates when Simon collapsed and came running back in to call for help.

| Clue? | Rachel attacks Marcel who is threatening to tell the truth about the bribery she arranged for Simon- he is a witness. |

So, there we are – five suspects. Now to select one and make them into the real killer.

HOW TO WRITE THE FIRST DRAFT OF A COZY MYSTERY	
1	Expand the 3 Hooks and a Sleuth idea.
2	Decide on your Target Wordcount.
3	Consider what Point of View you want to write in.
4	Create a Memorable Sleuth.
5.	Who is the First Murder Victim?
6.	Who are the Possible Suspects?
7.	Character Development for the Murderer.

STEP SEVEN. The Murderer

The character development for the murderer should be as vigorous and detailed as the development for the sleuth. After all, for most of the book, the sleuth will be reacting to the events that the murderer has set in place.

The murderer is essentially driving the plot!

That's why it is always worth taking the time to develop the character of your murderer so that you understand:

- why they killed this person,
- how they killed them and

- **how they planned to escape justice.**

For example. Was this murder something that the killer had been planning for a long time, or was it an act of sudden passion in the heat of the moment?

In Step Five, we started with the victim and explored everyone who would have a good motive for wanting to kill them. This builds up the list of possible suspects.

Now it is time to select one of those suspects as your killer if you have not already done so.

Next, we are going to dive deeper into that character so that when you come to write the scenes where the killer is being interviewed by the police or the sleuth, you have a good understanding of the kind of dialogue the killer would use and how they would deflect the questions away from them based on their character.

Let's follow the case study and ask key questions about why this suspect is our killer, what their motivation is, and how they carried out the murder.

And the suspect I have selected to be the real killer is....

Case Study Worked Example from Spite Pairs with White

Suspect 5 – HIDDEN SUSPECT

Rachel Ellis. Office manager for the Kingsmede Wine Growers Association

Motive: Retribution and passion.

Secrets that will be uncovered by the sleuth.

Rachel Ellis has been Simon Fraser's mistress for the last 8 years and he kept promising her that they would marry one day. Simon went back to his wife Margot when his business collapsed but he kept seeing Rachel in secret. Simon told her that they would get back together when things were settled but she would have to be patient.

Rachel was an executive PA in the city. Met Simon at a charity corporate event that she had organised. When Simon moved back to Kingsmede, Rachel followed him and took a job working for the Wine Growers Association.

What is her backstory?

Simon arranged to meet Rachel in a hotel in London and asked her to help him. It is his burning ambition for his wine to be on supermarket shelves, but he needs to win the best wine of the year award before he can negotiate a big order.

Simon asked Rachel to invite Marcel Dubois to be the guest judge at the Kingsmede Wine Festival that year. Marcel owes him a favour and has already agreed that he will make sure that Simon wins the award.

Rachel is not happy with cheating, but Simon convinces her that this is what they have been waiting for. Their chance to be together. So, she agreed and set the whole thing up. The other two judges are not very experienced and in awe of this famous French champagne expert.

Why now? Simon has dumped her for someone else and is leaving.

RECREATING THE SEQUENCE OF EVENT ON THE DAY OF THE MURDER OR MURDERS

Learn how to plot out the events that led to the murder and what the killer did next.

What clues did they leave for the sleuth to discover?

- On the morning of the Wine Festival, Simon dumped Rachel.
- Simon has not been at the winery for months and not contacted her once.
- Rachel cannot believe it and argues with him, but it is no good. He plans to divorce his wife and marry his super-rich American girlfriend.
- Tells her that he is bored and needs new excitement in his life.
- Rachel is in shock and has to go outside to try and recover.

- Rachel realises in that moment that she had been used and conned like his other girlfriends. Everything Rachel had sacrificed and worked so hard to achieve is wiped away. It is too late to stop the Wine Festival, but she can do something to make Simon regret treating her like dirt.

Means

She goes back into the kitchen and adds smooth peanut butter to the special plates of gluten-free canapes in the kitchen, wraps and labels them very well and leaves them in the kitchen for Erin to collect. Simon has ordered gluten-free food that day.

Opportunity

Rachel was responsible for organising the Wine Festival, so she is a familiar face.

She offers to help clear the tables when the awards are just to be announced. Simon has already eaten most of the peanut canapes, but she casually slips the few leftovers into a napkin and takes them out to the kitchen and crushes them into the bin.

Then she puts on her smart black suit jacket in the kitchen and goes back into the room to join the organising committee.

Alibi

She had already left the room with a tray of glasses and plates and was in the kitchen when Simon collapsed.

How is she caught?

Link to the Second Victim: Marcel DuBois

Rachel attacks Marcel at Roger Fitzpatricks's vineyard.

Her plan is to frame Roger for killing wine judge Marcel out of revenge for losing out on the wine award.

Her Motive for trying to kill Marcel?

- Marcel wants to confess and go to the authorities.

- Marcel feels totally guilty about what has happened and tells Rachel that he has decided to go and see Roger at his vineyard that evening and confess that Simon did pay him to get the award. Then they can go to the Wine Association together.
- Rachel cycles to the vineyard and meets Marcel. Tries to persuade him to change his mind. *Nobody knows. They can keep this their secret.* But he refuses. He likes Roger and his daughter Amy. They deserve to know the truth.
- In that moment Rachel decides to silence him, and as Marcel walks away from her down between the vines, she smashes a wine bottle from her rucksack over his head, knocking him to the soil.
- But before she can hit Marcel again, she is interrupted by Amy coming back to the vineyard early with Erin.
- Rachel escapes through the woods at the back of the vineyard on her cycle and rides quickly back to Kingsmede as though nothing had happened – making sure that she is seen by several people who can act as her alibi.
- The problem is – Marcel was only knocked out. He can identify her. What does she do now? The stakes have suddenly become a lot higher.

Now the fun can begin. Plotting out ideas for how my sleuth, Erin Kelly can work out that Rachel is our killer!

Story Development Exercise. Character development for the murderer

Which one of your suspects is the real killer?

The name of the killer.	
Motivation	
Secrets and backstory that the sleuth will uncover	
Why now?	
Recreate the sequence of events that happened on the day of the murder (s)	
Means. How did they carry out the murder?	
Opportunity	
Alibi	
How are they caught?	

	HOW TO WRITE THE FIRST DRAFT OF A COZY MYSTERY
1	Expand the 3 Hooks and a Sleuth idea.
2	Decide on your Target Wordcount.
3	Consider what Point of View you want to write in.
4	Create a Memorable Sleuth.
5.	Who is the First Murder Victim?
6.	Who are the Possible Suspects?
7.	Character Development for the Murderer.
8.	Use Scene Cards to write a "discovery" first draft of Act One.

STEP EIGHT. Use Scene Cards to write a First Draft of Act One.

CONSOLIDATE YOUR STORY IDEAS

- You know who the first murder victim is and the means of death.
- You have a list of five suspects who all have valid motives, means and opportunities for killing the victim.
- You know which one of the suspects is the killer.
- You are now ready to recreate how the first murder was committed and then create the clues and revelations that will lead the sleuth to the killer. Add in possible fake clues and distractions from other suspects.

Build a simple Story Map for the first Sequence of Scenes before you start writing.

Creating an outline for your book may be new to you.

I prefer to consider the outline for the first draft of a new book as **a story map.** A pattern of steps which will lead you safely down a winding track through a thick forest and allow time for interesting diversions onto sideroads.

Story mapping makes it possible to:

- Start a new mystery and know that you are going to finish it. No more worry about having nothing to say or that your idea will falter and die after a few chapters.
- Give you a super quick start to writing the first few sequences which will automatically trigger your imagination to create the subsequent scenes and then the ones after that.
- Have confidence that you can dive into the writing and produce words FAST!
- Be completely flexible about how your sleuth is going to get involved in the murder investigation and then stay locked into a story situation where you can throw rocks at her.
- Accept that you don't know how your characters are going to react to all of these rocks. You can't know until they reveal that to you in the writing.

- Be open to new situations and diversions at any time. These are points on a map, not a fixed route you have to follow.
- Give yourself permission to write a rough draft which will not be perfect, but it will reveal what you need to know to edit it when it is complete. Perfectionism can kill if you let it. Think of this draft as an experiment and a piece of fun writing.
- Nobody will see this draft. You can write what you like. Your words will not be examined and judged and criticized. Write it in any tense you want. First person point of view? Great. We love to get inside out character's heads. Switch to multiple points of view later? No problem. Let the sleuth and the murderer explain how they are feeling.
- You will know that you will not fail. You are going to follow a story pattern which is as old as human nature. A pattern which meets the expectations of anyone coming to enjoy a cozy mystery story.
- You are going to enjoy writing because you don't know what it is going to happen with these characters as they start the investigation. That way it stays fresh and interesting.
- Turn off your internal editor and nasty nagging limiting beliefs long enough to write faster than you thought possible and enjoy it. You can write the scenes out of order or work backwards from the end. It is up to you.
- The story magic happens when you step off the tarmac and onto the dirt track which leads towards the magic forest.
- You can still see the road if you look over one shoulder and that gives you the confidence and the freedom to explore as much as you want and learn new things about the characters that are walking by your side.

Now for the fun part. Writing and experimenting with the text of the opening scenes of Act One.

Noting down the plot outline for the opening scenes of your novel need only take a few minutes but it will give you confidence that you can complete the work and enjoy doing it.

The opening scenes have to accomplish a great deal in a limited number of words. This is tough to perfect in a first draft, so be kind to yourself and accept that your first chapters are going to be heavily edited later.

Sketch a very basic bullet point outline of the opening sequence of scenes from the sleuth's point of view.

The goal is to jot down the steps the sleuth is going to take, starting in their ordinary world, then moving to the point where the sleuth commits to investigating the murder at the end of Act One if you are using the Four Act Story Structure Model for the murder plot.

Start filling out some of the detail for every scene as ideas emerge as you think about the content these scenes. Don't worry if they are only snatches of dialogue and ideas for settings etc.

The goal is to have at least a few pages of notes, ideas and bullet points about the plot, dialogue and what could happen for every scene in this working draft of Act One.

The characters drive the direction the story will take.

I start with a solid outline for Act One of a Four Act novel, then take what I have learnt while writing the opening scenes to build a basic road map for the rest of the plot using one-line ideas for the remaining 12 specific turning points in Acts Two, Three and Four of the story.

This process means that I am open to any new ideas that come along when the characters are on the page acting and reacting to the events and interaction with other characters. The character ALWAYS determine the direction the story should take, so focusing on the opening chapters is the quickest way to get into the plot.

This outline could be in the form of bullet points or a few lines of ideas and dialogue or possible conflicts, secondary characters, and settings. Whatever works for you and your process and your particular story.

I already know that these ideas will change or be replaced with something better, but they give me a basic outline from which to write the discovery first draft of the book.

I know where the story *could* go and I am excited about taking it there, or somewhere even more exciting.

Yes. This means that the first draft of Act One is very much a "discovery" draft, and that's okay.

Then you revise heavily after you have written the entire first draft of the book, to shape the words into the best version of your story so that the words on the page match your intentions.

I know that I will have to go back and change the opening scenes if the new ideas that emerge are even stronger than the original idea.

And that is precisely how it should be. I know that I tend to overwrite so some of those words will have to be cut, but that's okay too.

Yes. This is the quickest way to get the first draft of the story down.

Yes. This process is totally flexible, and you can adapt it to any fiction project.

Yes. It combines the benefits of plotting an overall outline using a 16-step story structure with the momentum and energy of intuitive writing or "pantsing" your way into your book.

No. I am not saying that this process will work for everyone, but it is the fastest way that I have come up with to break through the planning procrastination terror and actually start getting to know your characters in action.

Other authors underwrite the first draft and add extra layers, entire new scenes and chapters in the second draft based on what they have discovered while writing the first draft.

But it all starts with the opening chapters.

Combine the Story Idea with the Character Idea and get your main character onto the page and inside that story world – then introduce the murder.

What is a Scene Card?

A scene card is piece of scrap paper, postcard, or large sticky note where you write down your ideas about what needs to happen in each particular scene.

The scene cards I use have the following information:

Location or setting:

The key characters in this scene:

The three things that need to happen in this scene:

#

#

#

The Turning point at the end of the scene:

Scene cards can be a great plotting tool when you need to move ideas from inside your head onto paper. They can be moved around, scribbled on, thrown away and replaced and it only takes a few seconds to jot down the information.

The goal is to expand your outline ideas for this part of the story into scenes using simple bullet points so that your story builds into sequences, scene by scene to achieve the 'rising action' as stakes and tension increase until the final battle between the sleuth and the killer in Act Four of the book.

Scene cards are not written on tablets of stone. They are intended to be discarded and replaced with stronger ideas which will emerge from the writing, but we all have to start somewhere with a quick note about what could happen at this point.

Worked Example of a Scene Card from the Case Study.

> **Location or setting:** At the wine festival.
>
> **The key characters in this scene**: Erin, Prisha, Simon Fraser
>
> **The three things that need to happen in this scene**:
>
> # Erin is serving her canapes, and Prisha is waiting tables.
>
> # Introduce her pal Amy and her father who is a rival winemaker.
>
> # Simon Fraser arrives and argues with his son.
>
> **The Turning point at the end of the scene**:
>
> Simon collapses due to nut allergy.

Don't worry about whether this text will end up in your final manuscript or not. This is play time using free writing as an experiment to get the "feel" of whether this character is someone you like and want to spend time with for the next few weeks or months.

If they are? Great. Stay with them after you have completed the opening sequence of scenes and use their emotional conflict to sketch out the rest of the story.

But if you are not interested in writing about this person, then this is the time to find out. Scratch that idea and go back to the beginning and redevelop your character.

You can save a lot of time and wasted energy by triaging your story idea at this stage before you dive into the remaining three quarters of the book!

Now It's time to get creative and start writing the scenes leading up to the discovery of the first murder victim and then the reaction to the death.

SKETCH OUT THE OPENING SCENES

1	**Outline how the first murder victim is discovered and the means of death.**
2	**Develop the list of 5 suspects and their motives, means and opportunities.**
3	**Select one suspect who is going to be the main antagonist and an equal match for the sleuth. Build up their backstory.**
4	**Recreate how the first murder was committed and then create the clues that will lead the sleuth to the killer. Add in possible fake clues and distractions from other suspects.**
5	**Start filling in the outline text of Act One with expanded scenes and dialogue.**

What is your ultimate goal for these opening scenes?

#To create a charismatic and interesting sleuth who arrives onto the page as a real person. Imperfect. Flawed. Opinionated and strong.

 # Your sleuth does not come into the storyworld alone. He or she will have ongoing relationships, positive and negative, with family, friends, and members of the local community.

Every one of these secondary characters adds richness and depth to your story. Family members should add a range of different emotional responses, perhaps warm, witty, or exasperating, as do physical settings.

Incorporate some familiar elements into the storyworld.

I believe that this is one of the reasons why culinary and pet cozy mysteries are so popular – the setting brings a sensory and comforting element to the mystery story and grounds it in familiar physical attributes.

Let the characters describe the location in detail. The reader should be able to visualise the setting in colour, smell it and almost be able to touch it.

#This is meant to be light entertainment with humour and heart to balance out the murder investigation. There is nothing wrong with escapism that makes us smile.

#This is not a spy story, or a cop show packed with forensic gory details, violence, and shoot-outs, although there are interactions with police, and they do resolve crimes.

It is more about family and interpersonal relationships.

ACT ONE – Reminder of the Key Story Beats in Act one

Sequence 1. Ordinary world and introduction to the Sleuth

Sequence 2. Conflict and the Inciting Incident.

Sequence 3. Reaction to the crime.

Sequence 4. A commitment to solving the murder/crime – the clock starts ticking now. The game is on!

These were described in detail in the Section of Cozy Mystery Story Structure, so I am going to summarise the key points you can use on your Scene Cards.

Act One. Sequence 1. The Sleuth in their Ordinary World

Characters and world building

Introduce one main character in their story world and give the reader a few pages to get to know them. It doesn't matter if it is historical, paranormal or contemporary as long as the worldbuilding feels real and engaging.

Who is the sleuth?

Can the reader recognise themselves in this character and relate to them?

#Hook. What makes this person cool, interesting, and different?

This is linked to the theme of your cozy mystery. Culinary, hobbies and crafts, animals or paranormal. What makes this character different?

#Hook the reader in the first paragraph by hinting at a turning point or crisis in her life. Give the reader some reason to root for this character.

#Who are her friends and family and sidekicks our sleuth is going to talk to and hash things out with? Can you introduce these in the opening scenes?

#Establish the setting, period, tone, style, and point of view of the story. By the end of the first scene the reader should know precisely where they are and can visualise the setting. This locks them into the world stage on which your story will be played.

#Consider what point of view (POV) would work best for this story. Many cozy mystery authors use first person POV for the sleuth from the start, so the reader is immediately inside the head of the character who they want to follow in this story and possibly more in the same series.

By the end of the first chapter, the reader knows precisely what kind of mystery this is, who the main character is and what the stakes are if they mess it up. Then you can get to work on the crime and mystery storyline.

Act One Sequence 2. The Inciting Incident

This is the starting point for the murder mystery, even if the incident is a crime that is linked to a murder that takes place later in the book.

The Inciting Incident is the first significant event that completely disrupts the characters life and spins it in a new direction.

In a cozy murder mystery it is more likely to be the discovery of the first murder victim.

The most common technique for grabbing the attention of a reader is through the use of curiosity.

Most successful mysteries begin by posing a puzzle to the audience, raising questions in their minds, and promising an answer.

That first question is triggered by what happens in the Inciting Incident.

- Something happens which throws the sleuth's world into turmoil. It could be a murder/attack or some shocking crime.
- Scene where future victim interacts with suspect – or show the body.
- Why is she involved in this murder investigation? Is she a suspect or is a relative or friend a suspect? Did she discover the body?
- WHO IS THE SIDE KICK or sidekicks who she is going to talk to and hash things out with? They should have the skills and local knowledge that the sleuth does not have – and can add a touch of humour and quirky mannerisms or even add a bit of conflict into the investigation.

Who is the first murder victim?

Take time to explore all of the possibilities from your one-line entry in the three hooks and a sleuth writing exercise and then the expanded book description.

- Who is your first victim?
- Where is the body discovered or has it been hidden?
- How were they killed and why?
- The suspect's motives are influenced by the character of the first victim. Why did someone want to kill this person?
- Is there going to be a second victim? How were they killed and why? Is it the same killer? Make notes for the next murder victim as you work on the first.
- Does the sleuth know the victim – this gives her a reason to get involved and care about why this murder happened?
- Is this first victim likeable? Uncover a backstory – victim has been leading a carefully constructed lie.
- Are they unlikeable? We have to make the reader care that this person has been murdered. Give them personality. Give the reader some insight and connection with the victim.
- The victim knew the killer.
- Means of death should not be too gory.
- Is there any special knowledge required which will lead them to the killer?
- Who has the means to carry this out?
- Who had access to the victim at the time of the murder?   Means. Motive. Opportunity.

Act One Sequence 3. Reaction to the Murder

The sleuth has to try and deal with the problem of the inciting incident and is struggling to know what best to do and how to react to this disruption in her normal life. She probably does not want to get involved and refuses the "Call to Action."

Does the sleuth have a mentor or sidekick or friend?

The sleuth debates what to do with her sidekicks/pals or family. She might resist the call to adventure/getting involved in the crime at first— she is not the person to get involved. Introduce everyone who is in the B subplot story.

The sleuth tries to resolve the situation but is blocked.

Establish the stakes. What happens if the sleuth doesn't reach react to this incident? Who would care?

In a cozy this should be linked to the character relationships between the sleuth and at least one "stakes character" they care about. Link the crime to the personal backstory and internal needs of the sleuth so that it is personal.

That's why there are: 3 BUMPS and a PUSH.

Use the *three bumps and a push* tool to quickly sketch out why the sleuth does not want to get involved and what will make her change her mind.

The sleuth will have to react to two or three events, problems and challenges which bring her closer to committing to the investigation, until something happens which pushes her into the final decision.

Whatever happened at the inciting incident interrupts everything she had planned and causes conflict on multiple levels.

Act One Sequence 4. The Sleuth Commits to the Investigation

The murder has shattered the balanced and ordered life of the sleuth and the local community.

Some major new event forces the sleuth to take action which will directly impact their life. This is an unexpected moment where something shifts, and it becomes imperative for the sleuth to commit to investigating this death.

At this point the sleuth has to commit to solving the crime/story question.

There is no going back now. They are fully on board. The sleuth has no choice. They have to get involved. They must be strongly motivated and have personal stakes in the investigation. This turning point is often called the First Major Plot Point since the main A story of the murder investigation begins here.

The Main Dramatic Question is posed. Will the sleuth find out the truth about the murder of this victim? This is the point at which we "see" what will happen in the rest of the story, and we know the story will be over when the sleuth discovers the identity of the killer.

	HOW TO WRITE THE FIRST DRAFT OF A COZY MYSTERY
1	Expand the 3 Hooks and a Sleuth idea.
2	Decide on your Target Wordcount.
3	Consider what Point of View you want to write in.
4	Create a Memorable Sleuth.
5.	Who is the First Murder Victim?
6.	Who are the Possible Suspects?
7.	Character Development for the Murderer.
8.	Use scene cards to write a "discovery" first draft of Act One.
9.	Sanity check after writing the Opening Scenes.

STEP NINE. Sanity Check after writing the Opening Scenes.

Do you like this story? Is it going to be fun to write?

Can you see yourself building this into a series and living with these characters for months and possibly years?

If the answer is no? Put this idea to one side and move on to the next idea. You might come back to it one day and recycle characters into other stories.

If the answer is yes? Excellent. Then get to work on the investigation.

	HOW TO WRITE THE FIRST DRAFT OF A COZY MYSTERY
1	Expand the 3 Hooks and a Sleuth idea.
2	Decide on your Target Wordcount.
3	Consider what Point of View you want to write in.
4	Create a Memorable Sleuth.
5.	Who is the First Murder Victim?
6.	Who are the Possible Suspects?
7.	Character Development for the Murderer.
8.	Use scene cards to write a "discovery" first draft of Act One.
9.	Sanity check after writing the Opening Scenes.
10.	Write down Ideas for the next Key Plot Turning Points.

STEP TEN. Write down Ideas for the next Key Plot Turning Points

This is a great time to plot out the steps taken by the murderer throughout the story until the final showdown with the sleuth.

As you wrote the opening chapters, the characters should have emerged onto the page, acting, and reacting, talking, and taking decisions.

They may have been too shy to talk to you at first. Don't worry. This is normal.

I like to think of it this way.

Imagine that you are visiting a new town for the first time and staying in the home of people you have never met before face to face.

Of course, not everyone will tell you their deepest secrets and longings the first time they meet you, but as you get to know them and take the time to listen to their story, they will emerge and develop into people you like and want to know more about. Even the killer has someone who loves them.

As they reveal more about themselves, your ideas for the sleuth, the killer and all of the secondary characters and their relationships may well change. **In fact, it should change.**

Short novel – focus on the characters and the interviews with the suspects to build to big reveal and turn at the midpoint at the end of Act Two.

Longer novel – work in a second murder. Go back to the murderer. Why have a second murder? Why now? What was this victim going to reveal?

- Build on the murderer's plan. They are getting desperate.
- Did they leave evidence behind?
- Perhaps the first murder was planned but the second murder was a spontaneous decision.

- What does this second crime or murder reveal to the sleuth?
- Are the two connected and if so, what connects them?

This is a puzzle so all the pieces of the jigsaw must be there – including a few pieces which are true but intended to act as red herrings and distractions.

Act Two

Sequence 5. The Investigation Begins

Who are the investigators? Who is in Team Sleuth?

Clues and reveals at the murder scene. What clues did the murderer leave behind or what did they take with them?

Sequence 6. Balancing Sub-Plot

This could be a continuity story or romance layer.

Sequence 7. Motives and Secrets revealed.

The victim's lifestyle and why he may have been killed. Give them enough backstory to create four or five suspects who are motivated enough to kill the victim.

Sequence 8. Midpoint of No Return.

About halfway through the book there could be another murder or serious attack or other event around end of Act Two.

Short novel? Major clue or reveal that changes everything.

Long novel? Another death or attack that takes the sleuth in a different direction.

At this point I am jotting down notes and initial ideas for Acts Three and Four rather than plotting in detail. Better ideas may and probably will pop up during the development and actual writing of Act Two.

Act Three

Sequence 9. The Killer is Blocking the Investigation

Reaction to the midpoint clue or revelation or second murder. New clues and revelations must be investigated. New lines of information.

Sequence 10. More Complications. Stakes increase.

The killer is not going to go down without a fight. The closer the sleuth gets to the truth, the more the tension ramps up.

Sequence 11. Suspects narrowed down.

End of Act Three major turning point with a set-back. All looks dark, the killer has won. Why? What has happened?

Sequence 12. Apparent Defeat – all is lost. The killer had won this round of the fight and the sleuth is defeated.

Act Four

Sequence 13. Heroine sleuth gets her mojo back and is back on track.

Some new insights or revelations or clues that locks suspicion on one suspect.

Sequence 14. A New Action Plan

Sleuth has to come up with a plan to get to the truth.

Sequence 15. The grand finale.

One to one Final Battle with the real killer.

Sequence 16. Resolution

What does the ordinary world look like when justice has been restored? How is the sleuth different?

WRITING A CONTINUITY SERIES

WRITING A MYSTERY SERIES

Cozy mystery series have never been so popular.

Agatha Christie may have started the trend with Hercule Poirot and Miss Marple, but readers love returning to the same characters they have come to know, living real lives in this fictional world.

However, all of the wonderful elements of cozy mysteries that make this genre so attractive to readers, can also create problems if you are writing a series featuring the same main sleuth and sidekicks and set in the same community.

Building Layers of Conflict into your story.

In every cozy murder mystery there are five main storylines which you can use to generate the conflict in every scene that will keep readers hooked and turning the page to find out what happens next.

The Main Murder Plot.

The Main A Plot. This is the murder investigation that is specific to this story. Each book in a series will have one or more murders that create a unique murder mystery plot.

In a murder mystery, the overall goal is to identify the killer and bring them to justice. This is the spine and the desire line of the book that drives the action forward in every scene.

We know that the murder will be solved by the end of the book, but the goal is to create a clever puzzle and set the reader wondering how the sleuth will find the killer. What skills and techniques will the sleuth use?

What is the personal motivation that compels the sleuth to investigate this murder?

The reader has to believe that someone the sleuth knows and cares about is in danger and the stakes are high.

Then there are Four Continuity Sub-Plots

These sub-plots are all character driven, which provides layers of emotional depth to your mystery.

In some cozy mysteries one type may dominate, especially in romantic suspense, but if you are intending to write a series of linked books with the same sleuth and story world then all four types of subplot should be built into your story planning.

The Secondary Character Plot

This is usually a character-based subplot about a close family member, friend, sidekick, or a romance relationship that creates interest, conflict, and sparks for the sleuth.

The quirky sidekick, for example, is someone for the sleuth to spark ideas off. It could be a pet, ghost, senior relative etc. who is a great fit for your niche.

They are often humorous and intriguing, and they have their own backstory. Each of these secondary characters can become the main character in another book in the series.

Think about how Agatha Christie used the Captain Hastings character as a foil for the Belgian detective. He has his own money and a motor car at a time when that was relatively rare for most of the UK population and is able to take the "innocent and unknowing" approach to scenes and evidence. When a trained detective like Poirot explains something to Hastings, he is explaining his rationale to the audience of readers.

On the other hand, Hastings does not appear in every Poirot book and the focus is always on the private detective's relationship with the local police officers.

It is possible to have a multi-protagonist series where there are two or more sleuths working together to solve crimes and this can work very well, as long as there is one main character for the reader to connect with.

The Community Conflict Plot

This is your continuity subplot that will run for the entire series of books that you write in this story world. Can you come up with one or more characters in that story world that could crop up in every book in the series?

For example. This could be the disapproving family member, local police chief or member of the community. They are going to come into contact with the sleuth in some way in every book that generates conflict. You can build a situation where this antagonistic character has to come to our sleuth for help.

The Character Arc of the Sleuth

When you introduced your main sleuth in the first chapter of book one, in most cases they came on stage with a lot of emotional baggage and unfulfilled needs and wants. These are often linked to family and loss and absent parents or spouses.

You do not have to have character change over a series, but this adds interest, sympathy and empathy for that character and helps readers to engage with them as real people who are fighting to build their lives.

Over the course of the series of books, you can work on this internal conflict and show how the sleuth grows and "arcs" from book one to the last book in the series.

This is often linked to a romance subplot where each book in the series carries on the "will they/won't they" get together story thread that automatically creates emotional tension. Both the sleuth and the romance interest will have limiting beliefs and internal conflicts which will prevent them from being together.

The aim is to have your reader looking forward to the next book in the series so they can find out what happens next in this relationship.

The Setting and Storyworld

As a reader, I feel that I am coming back to a series to revisit a familiar world. The challenge with mystery series is that new characters have to be introduced into your small town or location to keep things fresh, while still being grounded in the same location.

Tourists, business contacts, regional fairs or some other public event or location are all ways that the sleuth can meet new characters. Dead or alive. This is one of the reasons why many cozy mystery sleuth are set in shops, libraries, wedding venues or work situations where the sleuth can come into contact in some way with the general public.

To prevent long series becoming boring, you can always send the sleuth away for a few days for a temporary break or a longer summer holiday, but always ground them in the familiar location that your readers have come to love.

Combining all Five Plotlines

The key thing is to weave these four types of subplot into the Main A plot storyline that is the spine of your book, in a way that feels organic and authentic.

At this point, you are probably thinking, hang on a moment, I have to handle five plotlines in a cozy mystery that might only be 50,000 words long?

Yes, you do. But it's okay. The secret in building up to that powerful reversal at the end of Act Three, and to incorporating multiple storylines, is to leverage the power of Story Structure we have already been working on.

As long as you keep the murder investigation as the solid spine of each book in the series, then you can weave in one of the other subplots which are all set in the same storyworld, with the same main cast of characters.

Create a Story Bible for the Book Series

If you are hoping to write a long continuity series of linked books, then it is always a good idea to collect together your notes and character profiles from book one before you move onto book two.

The last thing you need is for a reader to point out the sleuth's best friend and sidekick was described as a blond with blue eyes in book one and a brunette with brown eyes in book four!

Think of your series bible as a physical or electronic folder where you can save your notes and ideas in one central place where you can quickly find exactly the detail you are looking for, without having to read back through the mystery novels.

How much you note down and how you file it depends entirely on the kind of story you are writing and what elements are going to be carried over from book to book.

What should be in your Series Bible?

Details of each of the Main Characters.

Include a full biography including: age, physical characteristics, birthday, parent's names and where they are now, where they were born and educated, their internal and external conflicts, deepest secrets, goals, any favourite expressions that they like to use and how they speak. Are they introvert or extrovert? Chatty or quiet?

If anything new emerges as you write more books in the series, add these details to the profile for each main character. Perhaps they always drink tea and hate coffee. She is allergic to pet hair and loves house plants.

The backstory for these characters can emerge slowly and be revealed in the text as each book progresses.

Shorter Details for each of the Secondary Characters.

Where do they live and work and connect with the sleuth? Pull out the little details so that you can use them in the series.

If it helps your story, draw a timeline connecting the characters together.

For example, in book one, the main sidekick character decides to give up his office job and start a dog grooming business. In book two, he gets involved in a dog napping in his salon. Who are his family and how does he come to love dog grooming? Does he always have dog hair on his clothing? And the sleuth is allergic to animal hair.

A Timeline

The series is usually a continuation from one book to the next, so you should be crystal clear about the timeline for the characters and the events. Some authors start the next book only a few weeks following the end of the previous book. For others, it can be months, but rarely years. The character connections have to remain consistent.

The Setting.

This can be challenging since cozy mysteries can be set in any time period, and physical location, including paranormal, futuristic, urban, and rural settings.

If it helps, don't be embarrassed to draw a sketch map of your location, including where all of the major buildings are placed in this town and where the sleuth lives and works.

How long will it take her to drive home or walk to the office?

Does she pass other shops, bistros, and bookstores etc. or is it a seaside town? What is her view like?

Your accurate and sensory description of these settings will bring them alive. The reader should be able to taste the salt from sea spray or inhale the scent from the musk roses that grow around the door of the sleuth's cottage.

Paranormal Mysteries

If you are writing paranormal or supernatural cozy mysteries, record all the magical rules of this universe, the words the characters use to create spells and any magical systems and symbols. Are there new races and cultures to explore? How are they different from humans? How do they dress and speak?

Once you create the rules for this society, then you need to ensure that they are followed through in every book in the series.

Nostalgic Charm

There is one more component of the storyworld that is unique to cozy mysteries - the nostalgic return to traditional moral and social standards of behaviour and justice.

The reader is not coming to these books for a lesson on the statistics of drug-related city gang shootings. Instead, they want to be reassured that justice can be obtained through the deductive powers of people not unlike themselves, as opposed to shoot-outs and DNA analysis.

Good-hearted people bringing justice to a community.

These are escapist reads and every book in your series has to build on that foundation of intelligence and determination which is totally reassuring and comforting to the modern reader.

CASE STUDY DECONSTRUCTION

CASE STUDY MYSTERY
SPITE PAIRS WITH WHITE
BY SOPHIE BRENT

> Act One. Sequence 1. Chapter One/ Scene 1. Introduction to the Character in their Ordinary World.

SETS THE TONE for the entire novel. Hard or quirky, scary, or fun. Many authors use first person POV to get into the head of the sleuth as soon as possible and engage the reader with this character.

- **Introduce the main characters in their story worlds and situations.**
- **Let the reader know in the first scene/first chapter who the main character is and why they should care what happens to them.**
- **SHOW that she is skilled and has talents and strengths and can handle herself. She has to be intelligent and equal or better than the murderer.**

HOOK the reader in the first paragraph by hinting at a turning point or crisis in her life. Why is the sleuth at the end of their tether when the story begins?

Chapter One

ERIN KELLY SAT BACK in her hard wooden chair, stared at the computer screen, and realised that in all of the crimes against food that she was guilty of over her twenty-eight years, promoting a range of moulded chocolate party treats was probably going to cause her mother to stage an intervention.

She could almost hear her voice now. "You are a trained chef and sommelier! Why are you spending your time making chocolate boobs and baby rabbits?"

She had been forgiven for serving young Beaujolais with hake, the horrible mistake of unoaked Chardonnay with Kashmiri curry, and even giving into the client when they demanded Prosecco poured over their hot chocolate souffle, but this was the final straw.

Chewing her lower lip, Erin exhaled long and slow, rolled back her shoulders and half squinted at the website page.

The espresso and cream-colored banner splashed across the top of her new website proudly told the world that Kelly's Deli now stocked a full range of *Lottie's Luxury Party Treats.*

It was the shapes, of course. There was no getting away from them.

Okay, she had politely declined when one notorious hen party organizer asked her to make a special collection of cheeky anatomically correct body parts, but still, the new range was taking a risk. She really had to create an adult only option or face complaints from the fine citizens of Kingsmede, who were secretly ordering entire catering packs on the sly.

Behind Erin, her friend Carole stepped closer pointed to the screen and squealed in delight. "Oh, those are perfect! Fiona is eight next week and I promised my sister I would bring something special to her birthday party. Have you got anything left?"

"We sold out of most of the children's treats yesterday but let me just check to see if I have any animal shapes left." Erin replied in a singsong voice as she rummaged in the plastic crates. 'You are in luck. You can take your pick from milk chocolate teddy bears or mocha bunny rabbits. Oh, and a few very special chocolate dipped raisins. Except we call them rabbit droppings. Fiona would love that," she grinned. "I would recommend the rabbits."

Pulling out a flat tray, Erin stepped back and let Carol peer inside. Beautifully formed milk chocolate bite-size rabbits with pink tinted white chocolate ears stared back at them.

"Those look amazing," Carole said. 'I'll take the lot and two bags of the raisins."

"Hey! Steady. I don't want to be responsible for a troop of eight-year-olds high on organic chocolate and fruit puree!" Erin snorted.

"They can cope!" Carole laughed and then stopped and gestured with her head towards the deli. "Oh yes, I came in to tell you that Margot Fraser is here for the tasting. But you won't let her near those chocolates, will you? I'll fight anyone who even tries to take them off me."

Margo Fraser licked her lips and took another bite from her smoked salmon canape. "I don't know how you do it, Erin. I knew that the mini sandwiches and vegan crostini would be amazing, but these blinis are *so* delicious I could eat them all day. I certainly made the right choice coming to Kelly's Deli for the award ceremony."

"Well thank you, kind lady." Erin Kelly laughed and held out the edges of her apron in a mini curtesy before she sat down opposite Margot at one of her deli tables. "But that wouldn't leave any room for the dessert trolley. I tried several combinations of fruit and citrus to balance out your sparkling rosé before deciding on the gluten-free rhubarb and apple tartlets. The new recipe has a little more spice than my previous samples and I'd love to know what you think."

Margot flapped both hands towards Erin. "Pass one over and I'll let you know."

Erin's favourite customer stabbed at the mini tartlet on the selection plate with her cake fork. As her lips closed around the gluten-free pastry, her eyes fluttered closed and she nodded. "Gorgeous." She tapped her fork against the plate. "Simon has such a sweet tooth. He's going to love these. It's so difficult to find great desserts which don't contain nuts. Are those strawberry scones?"

Without waiting for an answer, Margot picked up a mini filled fruit scone and popped the whole thing into her mouth. "Oh yes. So good. The clients and growers will be thrilled."

A weight the size of a wheel of parmesan lifted from Erin's shoulders and she slowly settled back into the squeaky and cracked old wooden chair and allowed herself to relax for a few moments.

The aroma from the freshly baked bread and pastries cooling in the racks behind Erin's head mingled with the heady floral fragrance of Margot's perfume to create an almost overwhelming sensory overload.

No complaints! This was the price she had to pay for having the kind of sensitive nose and taste buds that could detect the subtle differences in flavour between the different Abbotsdown white wines that Margot was serving at the wine festival.

Margot Fraser had been coming to the deli for decades, but Erin still couldn't share just how long it had taken to create the range of nut and gluten-free canapes her father's friend was eating with such delight.

Yes, she was used to the 5am mornings but the relentless pressure of being both the chef and the owner was right there in the throbbing headache that she could not shake off.

Perhaps that was why her mother did not understand why she had chosen this life and was still gently nagging her to come and join the Rossi Catering Company in London or Florida.

Not going to happen mum. *Not going to happen.*

Erin grinned back and poured Margot another cup of her speciality fresh ground Italian coffee. "The Kingsmede Wine Festival has become a big deal around Hampshire. It was incredibly generous of you to sponsor the event this year. I know Rachel Ellis and the organizing committee are delighted."

Margot shook her head and waved her cake fork in the air. "Simon's quite determined to make a good impression at the Festival, so I was happy to get involved."

Then she shrugged her shoulders and gave a low sigh. "I may have been born and bred in Kingsmede, but as far as the locals are concerned, my husband is still a flash city banker playing around with winemaking as some sort of expensive hobby."

Margot took a sip of coffee, sighed in pleasure, and sat back in her chair, the exhaustion and frustration clear on her face. "Nothing could be further from the truth, of course. Simon has always taken Abbotsdown wine seriously."

"Didn't your parents plant vines years ago?" Erin asked. "I remember picking grapes at Abbotsdown when I was a teenager."

"Oh yes, it was quite the fashionable thing to do at the time. Shame that they were totally clueless about how to turn grape juice into something worth drinking," Margot laughed. "Simon had to basically start again from scratch."

Margot took another sip of the coffee. "I think that's why today is so important to him. This is his first real chance to show the other winemakers what we have achieved."

Glancing quickly from side to side, she bent closer to Erin. "A serious amount of hard work and money has gone into producing a sparkling reserve wine that we're all crazy about. Wait until you taste it! This is the start of something really exciting in Abbotsdown. I am so thrilled."

Then she grinned and pointed towards Erin. "Your food. Our wine. Knockout. He's bound to take the top prize today."

Erin sighed out loud with relief. The annual Wine Festival was the perfect opportunity she had been waiting for. This was her chance to show Kingsmede that Kelly's deli was the ideal place to go for all their party catering.

The last eighteen months since her father passed away had been tough. If there was any hope of building up the deli before her new bistro opened, she needed to work hard all summer to bring in more catering orders like this one. She already had orders from local hotels and pubs, but this was taking her catering to a whole new level. This was the kind of event she had been longing for.

She had to make it a success!

Suddenly Margot gasped, grabbed her lovely vintage handbag, and got to her feet. "Look at the time. James will be waiting for me at the airport and we're both going to be late if I don't get moving. He's flying back early after his month in Ibiza, so he probably won't be in the best of moods to start with. Thank you again for the lunch, Erin. See you this afternoon!"

"Best of luck and thank you again," Erin called out as Margot dived between the deli tables and with one wave of her hand in the air, she was out of the door and onto Kingsmede high street, leaving behind the faint aroma of fine fragrance, several empty plates, and a nice credit card payment for a two-course buffet for sixty guests. "Thank you very much indeed."

Erin was just about to start clearing the table when the cell phone in her apron pocket started playing one of her mother's favourite songs about when a moon hits your eye like a big pizza pie.

"Prisha Patel. You've been playing with the ringtone on my phone again, haven't you? Pest. Serves me right for leaving it around where you could find it."

"Who am I to resist temptation?" her best friend replied with laughter in her voice. "But I know that you are going to forgive me because I've got some good news and some not so good news on the catering front."

"Go on," Erin replied with the phone jammed under her chin so she could stack plates at the same time. "Let's start with the good news."

"Splendid choice. Are you ready? I've tracked down not one, but two, last minute waiters for the Wine Festival this afternoon. They're young, keen and cheap and I can pick them up in three hours."

"Two waiters? Okay, that sounds good so far. Now tell me why they are cheap. Wait a minute. Please tell me that they're not from that dodgy bar you took me to last week."

"Hey! That was a very classy hen night party and I've already told you that the boys got their underpants back at the end of the night. The other ladies thought that the dance routine was very tasteful, and they all enjoyed your chocolate treats. But you can relax. No way could you get those lads to wait tables for the pay you are offering." Then Prisha paused just long enough to make the hairs prickle on the back of Erin's neck. "The bad news is that they're two of my more interesting college students, but they were the only ones I could find at short notice."

Erin had a sudden flashback to the students she had met at the college graduation ceremony the previous year.

"Two of your students?" She winced. "Can you trust them?"

"They're going to be moving trays from one room to another. I hadn't realized that vocabulary and elocution were part of the job specification. You know you can't afford to be so picky. Not with this amount of notice."

"Not me. Margot Fraser. She's just been through every canape on the menu for this afternoon – again. There's a lot of pressure on her to make this event a success. I don't want to let her down, that's all."

"Well, that I can understand. Fear not, I know these two. They'll be okay. Just don't judge a book by its cover, that's all. Oops, have to dash. Bye for now! See you at the Festival. Bye."

"Prisha. What do you mean by that?" Erin stared at her phone in disbelief, then shook her head and chuckled to herself. Friends! She loved them all and she did need two waiters after the others cancelled on her, but sometimes…. sheesh.

The two last-minute waiters couldn't be that bad. *Could they?*

> **Act One. Sequence Two. Chapter Two/ Scene 1. At the Wine Festival**
>
> **MAIN ACTION at the start. What does the POV character want at the start of the scene? He has to be proactive and wants this thing desperately.**

Looks like we're running low on those little sandwich things," Prisha said to Erin as she walked up to the buffet table and plonked down an empty serving tray. "Who knew that wine drinkers like duck and spiced mango sauce rolls in July?"

"They're always a hit. The salty sweet taste is a great match for white wine."

Erin scanned the jostling guests from her buffet station at the back of the room, close to the kitchen and the side entrance to the car park. The Festival had officially opened an hour ago and the tasting room at the Abbotsdown winery was already packed out. This had to be one of the most popular Festivals that she had been to in years.

It was a good thing that Margot had arranged for generous portions. The last thing she wanted was to run out of canapes.

"The boys are keeping busy," Erin said as she nodded to one of her regular deli customers. "Thanks again for finding them on such short notice."

"You have to admit that the tattoos and black ear studs do add that certain contemporary ambiance to the event," Prisha smirked as they watched Wayne and Marlon stroll among the Festival goers. "Don't want to be all boring, do we?"

"Perish the thought," Erin nodded with raised eyebrows. "Lucky for us, Margot hasn't arrived yet. She must be waiting for her family to make their grand entrance."

Prisha looked around the room. "Good crowd though. Are they all here for the free booze?"

"Could be," Erin laughed and loaded up Prisha's tray with smoked salmon blinis and duck sandwiches. "Rachel Ellis has done a brilliant job promoting the Wine Festival. It's a shame that we are working. It's such a lovely warm afternoon, a glass of chilled champagne would go down very nicely."

"Not for me." Prisha winced and wrinkled her nose. "Champagne is all well and good, but I prefer a nice glass of Merlot."

"Wash your mouth out, Prisha Patel," Amy Fitzpatrick smiled as she came up to the table and gave Erin a one-armed hug. "We make our own sparkling wine right here in sunny Hampshire. Who needs Merlot?"

"Amy! When did you get back from France?" Erin stepped out from behind the buffet and gave her old school friend a proper hug. "I thought you were living the high life in some swanky chateau in Burgundy?"

"Two days ago. I managed to escape for a week before the harvest season, when the mayhem really kicks in. I could hardly miss the Festival, could I? My dad would never forgive me. "

Amy winked at Erin and turned around with a grin. "Looking good, Prisha."

Prisha glanced down past her crisp white blouse and black skirt, to the practical flat black trainers she was wearing. "In these shoes? You have to be kidding, Amy. But I can own the look. Good to see you again, girl." Then she picked up the tray and sauntered off into the crowds, stopping at every handsome male person in the room.

"Such dedication! She really has not changed one bit. What did you have to promise to persuade Prisha to be a waitress on a Saturday afternoon?"

Erin rolled her eyes and waved one hand in the air. "Emergency cover. The wedding season is in full swing, so Zoe is fully booked. Then Carol's mother sprained her wrist yesterday, so Carol's two cousins are working at her parents' pub for at least a week. The alternative was asking some of my cousins to help out and I don't think that the Kingsmede Winegrowers Association is quite ready for that yet. Lucky for us Prisha and two of her college students were home for the holidays and happy to earn some extra money. Ah here is one of them now. Marlon. Just the person I was looking for."

A tall young man in tight black trousers and an oversized white cotton shirt shuffled over to her. Erin took the empty tray from his hands and replaced it with a fully laden one. "That group over there need more smoked salmon blinis and crostini, and don't forget to offer them some crudites and grapes." Marlon responded with a small shoulder shrug but took the tray and strolled away at a snail's pace.

"I see," Amy said, "well at least the food is amazing even if the service is lacking!" She reached out, picked up a feta cheese canapé and popped it into her mouth with a satisfied grin. "This is delicious," she said between munching. "Perfect match for a dry white wine."

"Thank you, kind lady winemaker. I think you need some crunch with champagne and sparkling wines." Erin smiled and offered Amy a smoked salmon blini.

"Of course, I did have to sacrifice a lot of time sampling a full range of local sparkling wines to reach that perfect combination. It was hard work, but someone had to do it," Erin grinned. "I'm still experimenting with flavours and textures to build up the catering and food-matching side of the business, so I am hoping this is the first of many events. And wait until you see the dessert menu."

"What a terrible ordeal," Amy laughed. "Are the desserts still in the kitchen?"

"I am under strict instructions from Rachel Ellis that I can't bring the dessert platters out until after the award ceremony. Speaking of which, I'm supposed to serve Simon Fraser his gluten-free canapes the minute he comes in. Have you seen him yet? I've never seen the Festival so busy."

"Ah," Amy replied with such a note of such resentment in her voice, that Erin stopped what she was doing and turned to face her. "There might be a reason for that. Our host has invited a lot of his city banker friends and clients to spend the weekend at Abbotsdown. Apparently, Simon can't wait to show off his first release of a rose sparkling wine to all of his posh pals. Rachel is thrilled of course. She should get lots of free publicity in the trade press and hopefully serious orders from that crowd."

> **Conflict. Something blocks the goal and makes the character struggle.**

They stood side-by-side and looked out across the packed room of men and women in smart clothing who were clustered around the sampling tables, where local winegrowers were chatting with the guests and pouring wine into tasting glasses.

Amy gave a loud sigh. "You can imagine how thrilled my dad is with the new competition from Simon Fraser. One more city winemaker trying to make a name for himself by spending serious money on his latest hobby. He's convinced it won't last."

Outside on the patio, Erin could see that Amy's father Roger was chatting happily to the group gathered around his display table, which was already stacked with empty bottles.

"Is he worried?" Erin whispered as she loaded more trays with canapes, which were whisked away by the boys. "Your dad always wins the rose sparkling wine award. How many times is it now? It must be five at least."

"Don't let my dad hear you say that." Amy scoffed and leaned closer. "He has seven awards so far. The certificates are all lined up in the winery office. He is desperate to make that eight, so they look nice and neat on the wall."

Amy pushed her hands deep into the pockets of her smart trousers. "So yes, I think he is worried. We simply don't have the budget Simon Fraser has to invest in new equipment. From what I have heard, he is determined to put Abbotsdown vineyard into every major supermarket." She shook her head. "Simon needs to win this award even more than we do. No award. No supermarket deal. There's a lot at stake this afternoon."

> **Disaster. Failure and a serious setback. How do the stakes increase? The disaster provides the motivation to act and this has to be external, physical, and objective and real. Sharply defined.**

Erin looked around the room at the sampling tables.

"Wow. That is serious. There are a surprising number of vineyards around Kingsmede and they would all love to win that wine of the year award. I have to say though, this new visitors' room is stunning."

Erin gestured with her head towards the wide glass windows overlooking the neat rows of vines which stretched out towards the trees higher up on the chalk hill. Small bunches of round green grapes peeked out below bright green leaves.

"Not a weed in sight. I don't know how they do it."

"Manual labour," Amy snorted, "and not by the likes of Simon Fraser. He probably doesn't know one end of a grape vine from the other."

Then she paused and gestured with her head towards the stage which had been set up at the other end of the room. "Speaking of hard work, have you met the three judges yet? That's not a job I'd like. That back office must be a hotbed of pressure."

Erin peered over the heads of the cluster of chattering guests to the large room which had been laid out for the judges.

"Only for a few minutes," she smiled. "I took a plate of crudites and feta crostini through for the vegetarian lady judge and was scowled at by a grey-haired Frenchman. He murmured something under his breath in French about ridiculous food nonsense. From the sly looks he got, I think everyone in the room heard him too. It almost put them off the slurping and spitting."

"Ah. That sounds like the not so very charming Marcel DuBois. He's only here because Simon Fraser knows him from some sort of city club."

"Is that allowed?" Erin frowned. "I mean, the judges have to be impartial, don't they? If Simon Fraser is a friend of a judge he could be accused of favouritism."

Amy shrugged. "English winemaking is a small world where most people know one another. It would be almost impossible to find a judge who you have never met before. The other two judges don't have his experience for a start and... what's that terrible noise?"

Erin and Amy turned around and stared out through the open entrance into the car park, where a small two-seater sports car was racing up the lane, causing thick clouds of dust from the dry dirt road to rise up on either side. Guests walking up the grass to the tasting room wafted away the dirt as the car screeched to a halt next to a bright red convertible, where Simon Fraser was standing deep in conversation with a tall, younger man.

Erin sighed in relief. Simon has made it, which meant Margot would be right behind.

Simon was meticulously dressed in a very smart suit and matching shirt and tie, which to Erin looked way over the top for a country Wine Festival. He even had a very smart laptop bag hanging over one shoulder. From the expression on his face, he was not particularly pleased to see the new arrival and even less pleased when the driver slammed his car door, strode over and roughly grabbed his arm.

"Wait. Is that Simon's son? I hardly recognized him." Erin asked Amy as she peered out into the car park.

"The one and only James Fraser," Amy nodded. "Last I heard he was spending the summer in Ibiza on the clubbing circuit. It looks like he didn't have time to change. Stained chinos and a sweaty tee-shirt won't go down too well with his parents, especially not today of all days. Oh, and now they're fighting. Lovely! That's just what we need."

"Not now. I'll explain back at the house. Later." Simon snapped in a voice which was loud enough to be heard by the clusters of guests, who were streaming past them in the car park. "We'll talk when I'm ready. Not before."

Simon brushed his son's hand from his arm and walked in through the main entrance, followed by the younger man who he had been chatting to.

Amy gave a low gasp. "So, it's true," she whispered, and her shoulders slumped low.

"What's true?" Erin asked. "Do you know that man with Simon?"

"Only by reputation," Amy turned away from the door. "Sorry Erin, I need to go and find my dad. Catch you later." Then without looking back, Amy marched swiftly across the room and stepped out onto the wide patio overlooking the vineyards. Erin watched in concern as Amy strode up to her father and whispered something in his ear. Judging by the furious expression on Roger Fitzpatrick's face, this young man was not good news.

> **Reaction.** The emotional reaction to the set back.

> **Character is thrown off balance, hurt and upset. HOW to show this? Alternate between what your POV character sees/ sensory details - the motivation – and then what he does – the reaction – in response to that motivation. Can shift more than once. Describe the reactions from the fastest time to the slowest.**

Erin had no time to think about that. Simon Fraser had arrived. It was show time!

Reaching under the counter, she brought out the special floral plate of gluten-free canapés that Prisha had brought from the kitchen ten minutes earlier. It only took a few seconds to strip away the shrink wrap and add some fresh chilled seedless grapes to the plate.

Erin squeezed through the crowds of laughing and chatting people with wine glasses in their hands, towards the front of the room.

Simon Fraser was already deep in conversation with wine buyers as Erin approached the Abbotsdown sampling table. She couldn't help but overhear what his guests were talking about, as they twired and sniffed the sparkling pale pink wine in the tall champagne flutes.

"What a fantastic nose. I'm getting flower blossom followed by perfumed wild-strawberry compote with just a hint of vanilla and white toast."

"Wait until you taste it!" Simon replied with a laugh and raised his champagne flute in salute. "It's taken five years with new vines, but I think it's a winner!"

"I admire your confidence Simon, but the best sparking rose award has gone to Roger Fitzpatrick for so many years now. Roger has to have experience in his favour."

Simon lifted his glass towards the guest. "I strive for the best in everything, including winemaking. Perhaps Roger has become a little complacent. We'll have to see. The award ceremony should be starting anytime soon."

Erin waited a few seconds for the guests to move away before stepping closer.

"Mr. Fraser. It's lovely to meet you again sir. Erin Kelly from Kelly's deli. As Margot requested, I've made you a special range of gluten-free canapes for yourself and your guests."

Erin presented the pretty fine china plate and pointed out each of the canapes in turn. "We have smoked salmon, mayo cream and damson jam on buckwheat blini. Feta, tomato and chickpea puree on crostini, and mini duck and mango sauce sandwiches. All gluten free of course." She waved towards the buffet table. "There's also a lovely cheeseboard, grapes, and crudités if you prefer an alternative."

"This looks excellent," he grinned, showing way too much of his artificially whitened teeth, then peered at the plate. "Smoked salmon," he nodded and popped a whole blini into his mouth. His eyes blinked as the rush of intense flavours hit him. "Wow, that's good. Interesting." And then he looked up at Erin and said, "I'll just take the plate with me. Oh, have to get back to it." Then he bit into one of the sandwiches, sighed with delight and raised his eyebrows as a salute, before turning back to chat with his guests.

> **Reflection. Let the reader take a breath. Then in a new paragraph.**

When Erin looked back from the buffet table a few minutes later, almost half the canapes on Simon's plate were already gone.

"You look happy about something. Got a hot date with a wine lover?"

"No Prisha. Not today. I just like to see people enjoying my food, that's all. Simon Fraser has just tried all of the canapes, and I intend to blow him away with the desserts. They will be begging for the recipes, but they will have to come to the deli to enjoy them."

"Ah. Now I get it." Prisha tapped the side of her nose with her finger. "Brilliant marketing for the expanded Kelly's deli and future bistro. I like it." Then she looked over Erin's shoulder. "Here we go. It looks like the main event is about to start. Best get the tables ready for the next course."

Erin started clearing the plates onto a trolley, then looked up as the chairman of the Kingsmede Wine Festival went to the front of the room and picked up a microphone. Standing next to Tom Lewis were the three judges and several bottles from each of the vineyards at the Festival.

Where were the boys? They needed to get to work.

She almost sighed with relief when she saw the event organizer Rachel Ellis moving quietly around the tables, clearing away the savoury canapes.

> **Intense emotional reaction and feeling. Give the internal reaction from your character.**
>
> **The reaction is internal and subjective and is experienced by the point of view character and therefore the reader. It is the immediate reflex action in response to the physical experience.**

"Ladies and gentlemen, can I have your attention, please? I just wanted to say thank you again to Mr. Simon Fraser for welcoming us to this wonderful new visitors' centre here at Abbotsdown Vineyard. It really is quite spectacular. Thank you, Simon."

Enthusiastic applause filled the room, as Simon bowed his head in acknowledgment and raised his champagne flute towards the stage.

"And now to the main event of the Festival that you have all been waiting for. It is with great pleasure that I introduce to you, Mr. Marcel Dubois, our guest judge for this year's Kingsmede Wine Awards. We're going to start with the sparkling wines and then move on to the table wines. Over to you Marcel."

The grey-haired Frenchmen that Erin had seen earlier stepped forward and accepted the microphone.

"Thank you, Mr. Lewis. Thank you. It is a great pleasure for me to be here today in Kingsmede. As you know I have a particular passion for champagne, so I am excited to discover some great sparkling wine is also being made outside France by those who share that passion." He paused and gestured to the two other judges. "Today we have tasted some remarkable wine, and also some disappointments, but we have all agreed on one clear winner."

Marcel reached into his pocket and pulled out a slim white envelope. A polite smile warmed his face. "It is my pleasure to tell you that the rose sparkling wine of the year award goes to.. Abbotsdown Vineyard Rose Reserve. Many congratulations to the winemaker, Simon Fraser."

> **Then Reflex action. Immediate and automatic built-in response.**

There was a stunned silence in the room for a few seconds before the applause and cheering started. Erin stood on tiptoe to see Simon Fraser and the young man he had come in with hugging and shaking hands. Other guests surged forwards, patting Simon on the back, and raising their glasses.

Erin was about to start applauding when she suddenly realized that there was someone missing.

Where was Margot? She should be here to celebrate this huge achievement. Her parents had been so passionate about the vineyard and they had all worked so hard to make it a success. She deserved to be standing on the podium with Simon, sharing the applause and the praise her husband was receiving.

Erin smiled around the room and then glanced back towards the kitchen. There was no sign of Margot, but her gaze locked onto Simon's son.

James Fraser was standing at the back of the room, glaring in fury towards the stage and apparently oblivious to everything else that was going on around him. James was the only person in the room who was not applauding his father.

Instead, his thin lips were pressed into a closed thin line and he was holding the champagne flute in his hand so tightly that Erin thought that it was going to shatter.

Suddenly the warm laughter in the room was broken by a harsh angry voice and Erin turned back to face the stage.

> **Physical response. Speech and motion.**

Roger Fitzpatrick had stormed his way forwards through the crowd and was grappling for control of the microphone with Marcel DuBois. Roger snatching it out of his hands and pointed one hand towards Simon Fraser.

"This is a joke, Fraser. A pathetic sham. We all know that you paid off the judges to give you the award. We don't need another city banker playing at being a winemaker. Go back to the city and take Hugo Brunel with you! You're not welcome here!"

> **Dilemma/ question. The character has to work through the difficult choices about what to do next. None of the options are good – they could be horrible.**

And with that, he threw the microphone onto the table and stormed straight through the crowd of people, not caring who he knocked into, and out into the reception area and the car park. And running after him, pleading for him to come back, was his daughter Amy.

Every eye in the room followed Roger and Amy in shocked silence until they were out of sight and people could breathe again.

> **New Decision or Action**

"Woot! Well, that's two down for desserts," Prisha blinked as she loaded more empty plates onto a trolley at the back of the room. "What got into Amy's dad?"

"He wasn't too happy with the result, that was certain. But right now, we have to get these plates back to the kitchen and serve the desserts before the next award is announced. Prisha? What is it?"

Prisha didn't answer for a few moments. Her attention was totally focused on the small cluster of people who had gathered at the front of the room. Then she beckoned to one of the waiters. "Marlon, over here."

> **Final sentences with character related twist to the next scene or chapter. Create a page-turning hook.**

The tall slim teenager walked back to the buffet table but kept looking over his shoulder. "What's going on?" Prisha asked him and gestured with her head towards the front of the room.

"That bloke who won the award. He was just laughing and then sorta grabbed his throat and went all red and fainted or something. It was weird."

Erin was just about to reply when there was a blood-curdling scream from the front of the room. "Call an ambulance!" a woman screamed with real panic in her voice. Then Rachel Ellis's voice called out. "Is there a doctor here? Does anyone have an adrenaline injection? Please! We need help."

Erin and Prisha put down the plates and followed the crowds as they surged forward.

Simon Fraser was collapsed onto the floor, lying on his side, with his legs raised towards his chest. His face and hands were flushed red and blistered. And he wasn't breathing.

This is the **INCITING INCIDENT** when Simon Fraser collapses. it comes it at around the 13% mark in this story and marks the end of Sequence Two in Act One. The remainder of the deconstruction will track the outline of the entire plot, sequence by sequence, without the text.

Act One. Sequence Three. Reaction to the Inciting Incident. 3 Bumps.

Erin knows that none of her food contained peanuts and Margot tasted them all personally, but she is immediately under suspicion since the victim collapsed immediately after eating her food.

Bump 1. Marcel, the French wine judge accuses her of poisoning the victim.

Bump 2. James Fraser, Margot's son, accuses Erin of killing his father.

Bump 3. One of her regular clients cancelled her catering order for the coming week.

Act One. Sequence Four. Commitment to the Investigation. The Push.

Push. Erin goes to deliver food to Margot's house and talks to James and Margot Fraser. Margot begs Erin to discover the truth about her husband's death and she promises to do whatever she can.

Act Two. Sequence Five. The Investigation Begins.

Erin hires her neighbour's nephew, Matt Ridley, who is a private investigator, to find out more about Simon Fraser and who would want him dead.

Act Two. Sequence Six. Balancing Subplot.

Erin and Matt go to interview Roger Fitzpatrick at his vineyard in the Hampshire countryside. Amy Fitzpatrick reveals that years earlier, Simon Fraser and her father used to be very good friends, but that all changed when Simon persuaded her father to invest in his business, which went bust. Simon left London in disgrace owing millions to his investors, including her father, who had trusted him and was left with nothing. The investors had been chasing their money for years without success.

Act Two. Sequence Seven. Motives and Secrets Revealed.

Matt and Erin go to the local hotel for lunch, but James Fraser has booked the dining room for his business guests. Matt talks to James to offer his condolences. James reveals that he had no clue that his father had sold the entire business without telling him. His father always carried an adrenaline injection with him because of his peanut allergy. So why was it missing at the festival?

Erin learns a crucial clue from her pal at the hotel. Rachel Ellis had lunch with Simon Fraser just before the wine festival and it was clear that Rachel and Simon were more than just friends.

Act Two. Sequence Eight. Midpoint of No Return

Matt agrees to find out more about Simon's business dealings. Erin talks over the case with her best friend Prisha and they meet Rachel Ellis outside her cottage. Rachel reveals that she is leaving the village for a new job.

Erin takes a call from Amy Fitzpatrick. She has just found Marcel Dubois, the French judge from the wine festival, knocked out and bleeding in her vineyard.

Act Three. Sequence Nine. The Killer is Blocking the Investigation.

Erin races to the vineyard in time to see Marcel being loaded into an ambulance. He manages a few words about Minta which make no sense.

Act Three. Sequence Ten. More complications. Stakes increase.

Amy reveals that Marcel wanted to buy their vineyard and had been there that morning trying to persuade her father to sell, but he had refused. Marcel had lost his estate in France in a terrible fire and wants to build his business with Margot and Simon Fraser. Her father still believes that Marcel was bribed by Simon to give him the award at the festival. Without that award Amy and her father have lost a major supermarket contract. But one thing is certain – Amy did not invite Marcel back to the vineyard. But someone lured him there.

Erin speaks to Margot Fraser and it is clear that she knew about her husband's many affairs and one was with a girl called Araminta. She also had no idea that Simon had not repaid Roger the money he had invested in the failed business deal and is determined to put that right.

Act Three. Sequence Eleven. Suspects narrowed down.

Margot and her winemaker go to see Amy and Roger at the vineyard. Someone called Marcel and asked him to meet them there, but it was a trap. Winemaker reveals that Marcel had signed a major contract with Simon on the day before Simon died – provided that Simon won the award. Marcel was bribed and realised that he had made a terrible mistake. Erin finds a crucial clue in the grass. It is Simon Fraser's adrenaline injection. Right next to some very distinctive footprints in the soft soil.

Act Three. Sequence Twelve. Apparent Defeat. All is lost.

Matt reports back from London that Simon Fraser was not trusted in the finance world and the latest rumour was that he was moving to New York to start a partnership with a pretty young finance lawyer. He was leaving Margot for good.

Erin heads back to the hotel to talk to her pal and it is clear that Rachel Ellis has already moved on and was cuddling up to James Fraser. Strange, considering how his father Simon had treated Rachel so badly on the day of the wine festival.

Erin goes back to the vineyard with cake from the deli and Margot is there, helping Roger and Amy to clean out the dusty wine shop. Constable Harris turns up and arrests Roger. Marcel has claimed that Roger was the one who attacked him.

Act Four. Sequence Thirteen. Sleuth gets her mojo.

Erin and Matt work through the case. Roger has an alibi for the time of the murder, but someone wanted to hurt Marcel and have Roger take the blame. The good news is that Matt has tracked down the mysterious Araminta.

Act Four. Sequence Fourteen. New Action Plan.

This is the clue they have been waiting for. Araminta is the real name of Rachel Ellis who left London five years ago and moved into their village at the same time as

Simon Fraser. Rachel is the key connection between both victims. Now they have to come up with a plan to trap her.

Act Four. Sequence Fifteen. The Grand Finale with the killer.

Reveal that Marcel has confessed that Rachel was blackmailing him. Erin and Matt meet Rachel on her daily cycle route and stop her with a fake story about a tribute for Simon Fraser. Rachel eventually confesses – Simon was hers and he betrayed her.

Act Four. Sequence Sixteen. Resolution.

Erin, Matt, and the team have a celebratory lunch at the deli.

***

Spite Pairs with White is Book Two in the **Kelly's Deli** series of contemporary culinary cozy mysteries, released in early 2021 under the pen name Sophie Brent.

SUMMARY

My goal with this book was to share with you everything that I have learnt on my journey to writing cozy mystery fiction, both in terms of what to write and then how to structure the text to create a satisfying experience for the reader.

As I said in the beginning of this book, there is no one-size-fits-all when it comes to writing fiction.

What works for me might not work for you.

This is completely to be expected. Every writer is unique and has to discover a technique and process that works for them!

If you are a planner by nature, my structured approach will immediately appeal to how you approach your writing. From personal experience, story craft can also be a great resource if you write intuitively and then come back to revise and rewrite the early drafts of your manuscript.

Many authors use a combination of techniques and create a simple outline or rough first draft as I have suggested, but then dive in and work on the individual scenes which could be anywhere in the story, slowly building rising action as they write from turning point to turning point.

No matter how you write, my sincere wish is that this book will be a useful guide to creating your own first draft of a cozy mystery and I would be delighted if you explored these techniques and tried them out with your next project.

Happy writing! Nina.

FREE BONUS ADDITIONAL RESOURCES

I know that many authors like to use a printable checklist of key story points or a worksheet when they are developing or editing a project.

This is why I have created two of the checklists from this book in PDF format. I hope that you find them useful.

You can download the PDFs at: https://ninaharrington.com/htwacm/

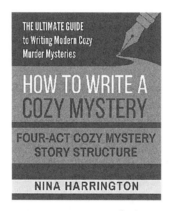

You can discover more resources for writers at: NinaHarrington.com.

THANK YOU

Thank you for reading HOW TO WRITE A COZY MYSTERY.

I love sharing my experience and information with other independent publishers like myself who are looking for the best way to share their work online but struggle with the overwhelming amount of information out there right now.

If you enjoyed this book and found it useful, I would really appreciate it if you would consider leaving a review of this book, no matter how short, at the online bookstore where you bought your copy.

YOU are the key to this book's success!

I read every review and they really do make a huge difference. Reviews help other readers to discover the kind of books and guides they want to read and is a great way to support authors.

Thank you.

ABOUT THE AUTHOR

Nina Harrington grew up in rural Northumberland, England and decided aged eleven that her dream job was to be a librarian because then she could read all the books in the public library whenever she wanted!

Nina writes fun, award-winning contemporary romance for HarperCollins, including the Mills and Boon Modern Tempted and Harlequin Romance lines. Almost two million of her books have been sold in 28 countries and translated into 23 languages.

The **Kelly's Deli** series of contemporary culinary cozy mysteries will be released in early 2021 under the pen name Sophie Brent.

Find out more at: https://ninaharrington.com/sophie-brent/

Nina is also the creator of the popular Fast-Track Guides series of books and online courses for writers. Find out more at: https://ninaharrington.com.

Made in the USA
Las Vegas, NV
21 August 2021